T0058163

# IS IT SAFE TO KISS MY CAT?

IS IT SAFE TO LOOK AT YOUR COMPUTER SCREEN?
IS IT SAFE TO CHEW YOUR PENCIL?
IS IT SAFE TO WEAR A BRA?
IS IT SAFE TO PICK UP A PIECE OF PAPER?
IS IT SAFE TO DRINK ORANGE JUICE?
IS IT SAFE TO SALT YOUR FOOD?
IS IT SAFE TO MIX YOUR DRINKS?
IS IT SAFE TO EAT A COCONUT?
IS IT SAFE TO WEAR HIGH HEELS?
IS IT SAFE TO WATCH TV?
IS IT SAFE TO USE EARPHONES?
IS IT SAFE TO DRINK HOT COFFEE?
IS IT SAFE TO WEAR FAKE NAILS?
IS IT SAFE TO NIBBLE ON YOUR NAILS?
IS IT SAFE TO DRY CLEAN YOUR CLOTHES?
IS IT SAFE TO SNEEZE AROUND YOUR DOG?
IS IT SAFE TO SLEEP WITH SNAKES?
IS IT SAFE TO RIDE IN THE FIRST CAR ON A TRAIN?
IS IT SAFE TO SIT IN THE PASSENGER SEAT?
IS IT SAFE TO READ A BOOK?
IS IT SAFE TO TURN RIGHT ON RED?
IS IT SAFE TO CROSS THE STREET?
IS IT SAFE TO EAT LICORICE?
IS IT SAFE TO COVER A SNEEZE WITH YOUR HAND?
IS IT SAFE TO STARE AT A BRIGHT LIGHT?
IS IT SAFE TO SHAKE YOUR DOCTOR'S HAND?
IS IT SAFE TO CLEAN YOUR EARS?
IS IT SAFE TO PEE IN THE POOL?
IS IT SAFE TO EAT ASPARAGUS?
IS IT SAFE TO SHOWER DURING A THUNDERSTORM?
IS IT SAFE TO WEAR FLIP FLOPS?

IS IT SAFE TO DRINK A LOT OF WATER?
IS IT SAFE TO LET YOUR DOG LICK YOU?
IS IT SAFE TO EAT OFF THE FLOOR?
IS IT SAFE TO USE HAND SANITIZER?
IS IT SAFE TO BLOW YOUR NOSE?
IS IT SAFE TO POLISH YOUR NAILS?
IS IT SAFE TO PEE IN THE POOL?
IS IT SAFE TO DYE YOUR HAIR?
IS IT SAFE TO EAT SPICY FOOD?
IS IT SAFE TO USE DEODORANT?

# IS IT SAFE TO KISS MY CAT?

## AND OTHER QUESTIONS YOU WERE AFRAID TO ASK

CAROL ANN RINZLER

ILLUSTRATED BY TIM FOLEY

SKYHORSE PUBLISHING

Skyhorse Publishing books may be purchased in bulk at special discounts for sales promotion, corporate gifts, fund-raising, or educational purposes. Special editions can also be created to specifications. For details, contact the Special Sales Department, Skyhorse Publishing, 307 West 36th Street, 11th Floor, New York, NY 10018 or info@skyhorsepublishing.com.

Skyhorse® and Skyhorse Publishing® are registered trademarks of Skyhorse Publishing, Inc.®, a Delaware corporation.

Visit our website at www.skyhorsepublishing.com.

10 9 8 7 6 5 4 3 2 1

Library of Congress Cataloging-in-Publication Data is available on file.

Cover design by Michael Short
Cover and interior artwork by Tim Foley

ISBN: 978-1-5107-2184-5
eISBN: 978-1-5107-2185-2

Printed in China

For my husband,
Perry Luntz,
Always.

And Katy the Cat, of course.

# Introduction

Catastrophes are terrifying, but most times it's the little things that do you in.

Consider earthquakes, tsunamis, and lightning strikes.

Scary, right?

Not compared to turtles, cats, and basketball.

In 2013, not a single American perished in an earthquake or a tsunami on United States soil. Twenty-three of us succumbed after being struck by lightning, a personal tragedy to be sure, but according to the National Weather Service, in any given year your own chances of being hit by a bolt of electricity is the proverbial one in a million.

On the other hand, according to the Centers for Disease Control and Prevention, that same year about 450 Americans, mostly children, ended with a *Salmonella* infection after playing with a pet turtle; 12,500, again, mostly children, developed cat scratch fever; and a whopping 500,000 United States citizens of all ages went to a hospital emergency room with an injury suffered while playing basketball.

Turtles? Cats? Basketball? It makes you wonder: If they're not safe, what is? Actually, nothing. As Jim Morrison and The Doors once sang to us, "No one here gets out alive."[1] But that doesn't mean you can't improve your chances to stick around as long as possible by following some simple rules to determine what's safe and what isn't, beginning with whether to kiss your adorable cat.

# 1
# ANIMALS

"Some people talk to animals.
Not many listen though. That's the problem."
—A. A. Milne, *Winnie-the-Pooh*

### Is it safe to kiss your cat?

You may think that Fluffy's performing intimate bathing rituals with her tongue makes mouth-to-mouth kissing a problem, but Paul Maza, co-director of the Cornell University's College of Veterinary Medicine health center, says that when she's done with her ablutions, fecal matter is swallowed and quickly disappears from her mouth. More to the point, most of the micro-organisms normally found in a cat (or dog's) mouth are similar to those in yours, including the bugs that cause periodontal disease in both pets and humans. The exception would be an outdoor cat who forgets to mention that she's been hunting and devouring small animals, which can add really unpleasant microbes to the oral mix. If your cat will sit still for it, brushing her teeth will reduce the bacterial population and her own risk of cavities and gum problems, but if you are truly uneasy about full-on kissing, a peck on the top of the head is perfectly satisfying. Ditto for dogs, Maza adds: "I kiss my dog all the time."[2]

## . . . to let your dog lick you?

Canines absolutely love to lick stuff, including you. Normally, that's a warm and friendly exercise, but you may catch a momentary case of the shivers when you read that one dog's lick passed a *zoonose* (an infectious disease that can be transmitted from animals to people) on to his owner. In 2016, the *British Medical Journal* (BMJ) published a report about a patient whose symptoms—slurred speech, headache, diarrhea, fever, failing kidneys—puzzled her doctors until they finally pinned it all on a bacteria called *Capnocytophaga canimorsus*. This bug, found in feline and canine mouths and nasal passages, is normally passed to humans via an animal bite; one of the doctors said it was only one of two such lick-transmitted cases he had seen in thirty years. The woman was treated with antibiotics and recovered. The BMJ does not report whether she still accepts a friendly canine lick.[3]

## . . . to let your pet chew your finger?

Human bites are often considered more serious than cat and dog bites, probably because human biting seems more unnatural and thus more aggressive than a nip from your cat or dog. The human mouth may contain nearly two hundred different species of bacteria, most of which flourish in that hard white tarter between the teeth. A bite that pierces the skin and draws blood may transmit these, plus a whole list of problems including hepatitis B, hepatitis C, the herpes simplex virus (HSV), syphilis, tuberculosis, actinomycosis, and tetanus.[4] What makes animal bites more troublesome is the fact that they are more common, particularly the nips most cat owners experience from time to time that may pass along cat scratch disease (CSD), which, in rare cases, may cause potentially fatal sepsis (blood poisoning).[5] CSD was first identified in the early 1950s. It took another thirty years to name the culprit, *Bartonella henselae*, a bacterium spread among cats by the cat flea *Ctenocephalides felis*. It took some more time to develop a diagnostic test and then to learn that related bacteria lurk in the mouths of other animals, including dogs. In the United States, the CDC estimates about twelve thousand cases of CSD a year, most commonly in the southern states among children age five to nine. As many as five hundred of these people experience symptoms such as inflammation in lymph nodes near the bite or the optic nerve, brain, bones, or heart serious enough to require hospitalization.[6] So kiss your cat (or dog), but don't annoy her (or him)—and check out "Is It Safe To Give a Dog a Bone?" on page 20 to see whose bite is most powerful or painful.

### . . . to scoop the litter?

Cats are finicky creatures that spend as much as 50 percent of their day cleaning and grooming themselves to stimulate the production of sebum, the oily substance secreted by the sebaceous glands that makes their coats shiny. Grooming also removes loose hair (oh, those hairballs!) and may even wipe away parasites on the skin. Obviously, any creature that obsessed with

cleanliness prefers a clean litter box. If you choose to ignore this truism, your cat will simply find another place to do her (or his) business. Scoop at least once a day to remove clumped urine and feces and keep your home free of the dreaded cat smell. Once a week, dump the entire boxful of litter into a trash bag, deposit the bag in a dump site outside your home, scrub the litter box with detergent, and then dry it with a disposable paper towel or let it air dry before refilling with clean litter. Be careful not to handle the contents so as to avoid contact with organisms such as *Toxoplasma gondii* (*T. gondii*), a single-cell parasite that infects a wide range of animals and birds but reproduces only in felines, both wild and domestic. Cats pick up *T. gondii* by eating infected animals, such as rats or mice or birds. Then they pass the parasite in their feces, so if you touch the waste you may end up with the *T. gondii* disease, toxoplasmosis. The Centers for Disease Control and Prevention note that more than sixty million people in the United States already harbor *T. gondii* but most never develop signs and symptoms of disease. There are, however, exceptions: infants born to infected mothers, people with a weakened immune system such as those with HIV/AIDS, cancer patients undergoing chemotherapy, and transplant patients who are taking medicines to lower the risk of rejecting the new organ.[7] Even if this is not you, the animal experts at *AnimalPlanet.com* recommend your wearing plastic gloves and maybe even a mask to prevent inhaling dirty dust while cleaning the box.[8]

### . . . pick up his poop when walking your pup?

Not just safe; considerate, as well.

### Dog Poo Haiku

Plastic baggie, in-
side out. Scoop it up, toss it
out. Save someone's shoes.

### . . . to fondle a fish?

Part of the pleasure we get from our pets is touching them to feel the silky fur or the smooth scales or feathers. But sticking your naked hands into the fish tank can be hazardous to your health.

First, some residents, such as the lionfish with its gorgeous multicolor spines, may puncture your finger, leaving a teensy wound through which bacteria such as *Mycobacterium marinum* can enter. This bug, a distant relative to the tuberculosis bacterium, flourishes in just about any confined puddle of water. Human *M. marinum* infection via any opening in the skin causes inflammation, may-

be *granulomas* (a bump of immune cells that fight infection and clump together to isolate foreign substances such as bacteria and fungi or even surgical stitches) or arthritic-like inflammation of the joints. Avoid the problem by using tools to rearrange tank "furniture." If you absolutely have to put your hands in to clean the tank, wear protective gloves and wash your hands afterwards lest the gloves leak around the wrist.[9]

### . . . to leave the cat in the room with the fish?

Cats are hunters. Fish are prey. If you've got both, watch out, particularly late at night when your cat, whose eyes have evolved to see well in the dark, is on the prowl for something tasty. You could

try training your cat to avoid the aquarium, but your best bet is to cover the top of the bowl or tank with something that lets air and food in but keeps the cat out. If the tank is sitting on a flat surface, surround it with crinkled aluminum foil that's uncomfortable for cats to walk on. When you leave the house, put the fish in a room with the door closed. If all else fails, it's time to choose your pet: one or the other.[10]

### . . . to touch a turtle?

Like snakes and lizards and other reptiles and amphibians, turtles may carry *Salmonella* organisms on its skin, scales, shell.[11] In 1975, to reduce the risk of infections due to pet turtles, the Food and Drug Administration banned the sale of those whose shell was less than 4 inches long. Following an increase in reptile-associated cases of *Salmonella* in Los Angeles linked

## Famous Names

Scientists often name newly discovered flora and fauna in honor of public figures. One such event occurred in September 2016, when a newly identified bug living in turtle blood was christened *Baracktrema obamai*. As the *Los Angeles Times* reported, this isn't just any old parasite. It is "so distinctive that it represents not just a new species but an entirely new genus."[14] Thomas Platt, a retired biology professor at Saint Mary's College in Indiana (and a fifth cousin, twice removed, of Barack Obama) who "discovered and named the flatworm to crown his career before retiring, has more than thirty new species to his credit. In the past, he's named them after his father-in-law, his doctorate adviser, 'and other people I have a great deal of respect for. This is clearly something in my small way done to honor our president,'" he said.[15] Obama already has a spider (*Aptostichus barackobamai*), a fish (*Etheostoma Obama*), and even an extinct dinosaur (*Obamadon gracilis*) named after him.[16] His reaction to the newest member of the menagerie was not recorded.

to pet green iguanas imported from Central America, a similar ban was imposed on the lizards.[12] The ban hasn't solved the problem. Nationwide between January 2015 and April 2016 the United States Fish and Wildlife Service, the United States Department of Agriculture's Animal and Plant Health Inspection Service (USDA-APHIS) and the Food and Drug Administration Center for Veterinary Medicine reported at least four outbreaks of human turtle-linked *Salmonella* infections affecting 133 people in 26 states, 54 of the victims children younger than 5.[13]

## . . . to share your bed?

There are an estimated 170 million cats and dogs in the United States. In 2011, the Centers for Disease Control and Prevention estimated that as many as two-thirds of them sleep in bed with their humans.[17] The benefits include a natural heating pad and the soothing sound of the animal's purring or breathing softly through the night. But parasites such as fleas may leap from pet to partner, some animal skin conditions are contagious, and  there's the issue of interrupted sleep. In 2013, the Mayo Clinic reported that as many as 10 percent of the patients at their sleep center complained of their pets' snoring, whimpering, moving about, and waking them (the patients) at night. "When people have these kinds of sleep problems, sleep specialists should ask about companion animals," says Dr. Krahn. One patient Krahn saw "owned a parrot who consistently squawked at 6 a.m. He must have thought he was a rooster."[18]

## One animal with whom you probably should not share a bed

Dogs and cats? Yes. Human babies? No. Each year, approximately three hundred infants die in bed with their parents when smothered accidentally by the weight of normal bedclothes such as sheets and blankets or by a sleeping adult's accidental rolling over onto the baby. The American Academy of Pediatrics says that to protect both infants and parents, babies should sleep in the parents' room but in their own bassinet, not in their parents' bed.[19]

### . . . to sleep with snakes?

So this lady walks into a bar with a python, no, actually she gets into bed with it. A few weeks later, she notices that her pet snake isn't eating and looks like it is losing weight. So the lady packs the python into a carrier and drives to the vet who has a scary message: The python, he explains, isn't eating because it is emptying its stomach in preparation for gobbling up its owner. Needless to say, the lady and the python went back to sleeping alone in their own beds.[20]

### . . . to share your dinner?

Despite that pitiful face staring at you as you eat and begging for a taste—or actually attempting to grab the food—no, you shouldn't

share your dinner. What you're eating may be good for you but not so great for your pet. For example, is there anyone who doesn't believe that cats love milk? Of course not, because they do. But cow's milk doesn't love them back. Animals are designed to flourish on mother's milk, and no cat (or dog) ever had a cow for a mother. Both felines and canines lack sufficient amounts of lactase, the enzyme required to metabolize lactose ("milk sugar"), so for them most milk and milk products are likely to set off digestive upset. The exceptions may be yogurt, cheese, butter, or ice cream— foods made by bacteria that split the lactose. If you are determined to enjoy the sight of your kitten, cat, puppy, or dog lapping her his or her milk, look for lactose-free animal products such as Cat-Sip® or Whiskas® Cat Milk at your friendly neighborhood pet store.

### . . . to feed your animal fruit and veggies?

Some plant foods are no-no's for your pet. For example, an avocado's flesh, leaves, seeds, and bark contain *persin* which is toxic for most animals—dogs, cats, horses, birds, rodents, you name it. Even a tiny taste of persin may lead to serious vomiting and diarrhea in dogs and cats; more can cause respiratory problems, inflammation of the mam-

mary glands, accumulation of fluid around the heart, and even death. Nobody knows exactly why grapes and raisins may trigger vomiting, hyperactivity, and kidney failure in some cats and dogs, but they do. Ditto for Macadamia nuts whose adverse effects include vomiting, tremors, weakness, paralysis of the hindquarters, and hyperthermia (fever) within twelve hours after eating. Raw, cooked, or powdered onions play havoc with your cat's red blood cells; two members of the onion family, garlic and chives, are likely to upset both Fido and Fluffy's tummy.

### . . . to put your pet on a raw food diet?

In the wild, lions and wolves and other carnivores eat raw stuff, but that may be one reason why they do not live as long as our companion cats and dogs. Imitating their natural diet by dropping some raw hamburger into your pet's dish may expose him to natural food-borne illness caused by contamination with naturally occurring *Salmonella* or *E. coli* organisms. "Raw food" products sold in pet stores are likely subject to "high pressure processing," a technique that reduces bacterial populations by sealing the food in packets and then compressing it.[21]

### . . . to give you pet a "wake-up" drink?

When your dog or cat seems slightly sleepy, you may think a sip of coffee or tea can deliver a wake-up call. Think again. The caffeine can trigger restlessness, rapid breathing, heart palpitations, muscle tremors, and seizures. As for tea and chocolate, along with caffeine they also contain theobromine, a stimulant that may trigger the same symptoms.

### . . . to hand out sweet treats?

Beware of xylitol, the substitute sweetener in some candy, chewing gum, and baked goods. This calorie-free additive may help you control your weight or cavities but it can send the insulin in your pet's body soaring, dropping blood sugar and maybe even leading to seizures and liver failure.

# Fat Cats & Pudgy Pups

Are you one of the several million Americans vowing to lose weight? If so, Nationwide, America's largest provider of pet health insurance, says you might want to invite your cat and dog to join you. 2015 was the sixth year in a row of rising pet obesity, doing damage not only to the pet but to the owners' wallets as well. Pet insurance holders filed 1.3 million claims for conditions and diseases related to pet obesity such as arthritis, diabetes, gallstones, and heart disease for which they were billed more than $60 million in veterinary expenses. Nationwide's sensible advice: save your money, save your pet, keep him (or her) slim and healthy.[22]

## . . . to let your pet taste bread dough?

Hard to imagine this happening, but if the possibility ever crosses your mind, ignore it. Yeasts work by consuming the sugar in flour and then releasing carbon dioxide (a gas that makes the dough "rise") and alcohol which gives the bread that "yeasty," beer-like aroma. If your pet gets some of the dough, the yeasts would do the same dance in her stomach, leading potentially to severe abdominal pain and/or inebriation.[23]

## . . . to share your bliss?

Dogs experience their very own bliss when you rub their tummies. They don't need your pot pleasure, but in New York City the incidence of canines (accidentally) making their way into their owners' "Mary Jane" rose nearly 150 percent in the five years between 2010 and 2015. In most cases, the symptoms—lethargy, wobbling gait, dribbling urine, salivating heavily, overreacting to sound and light and movement—are rarely life-threatening, so the standard treatment has been to induce vomiting if the ingestion is recent, and then keep the dog in a quiet place until the drug clears his system a few days later. (More serious poisoning may require more serious treatment including intravenous fluids, oxygen, and even ventilator/respirator support.) Note: Writing "dog" rather than "dogs and cats" is not a mistake. Dogs account for more than nine out of ten cases out of marijuana poisoning because, as one emergency room vet told *The New York Times,* canines will try anything once, sometimes twice, but, as every cat owner knows, "You never see a cat do that because they're smart."[24]

### . . . to give your dog a bone?

Not unless it's a plastic or rubber or artificial or treated one from the pet store. Canine jaws can make hash of even the toughest natural beef bone; cats can crack chicken bones in a split second. If they do, sharp splinters may run down into the gut, sending you and your pet to the animal emergency room.

### . . . to cuddle with a chicken?

The good news is a recent report in *The Malaria Journal* that says sleeping next to chickens can reduce your risk of catching malaria because the *Anopheles* mosqui-

toes that carry and transmit the disease appear to loathe the flavor and scent of chickens.[26] The bad news is that a new trend in backyard chicken coops, with humans living close to their chickens and ducks, has increased the number of live poultry-associated salmonellosis (LPAS) outbreaks in the United States. In the fifteen years from 1990 to 2005, there were seventeen such incidents. In the eight years from 2006 to 2014, that number more than doubled to thirty-six. Altogether, these 53 outbreaks made 2,630 people sick, 387 of them seriously enough to require a stay in the hospital where a total of 5 people died. The people most at risk were those who kissed their birds or kept them inside the house rather than in the backyard. The takeaway? Don't kiss your chickens good night when you tuck them into bed in their very own coops.[27]

## . . . to hold your horses?

Yes, but not too close. Horses may harbor a sub-species of the bacterium *Streptococcus zooepidemicus,* which may cause a variety of infections in the horse but normally does not affect humans. Occasionally, however, the bug ignores the rules and jumps species as it happened in the spring of 2016 when public health officials in King County (Washington State) were notified of two human cases. The first, Patient A, was a thirty-seven-year-old owner of a riding facility who groomed six horses and cleaned their stalls daily. When one of her animals developed a

# Crunch[25]

How strong are your pet's jaws? One measure is the PSI (pressure per square inch) exerted when the animal's jaws snap together. Exact figures are elusive because a dog or cat varies its bite from one situation to another, but several tests do estimate which beast has the strongest, most penetrating bite. A small animal, like a Yorkie, obviously exerts less pressure than a massive Mastiff, but like your cat's teeth, the Yorkie's tiny choppers are very sharp and pointy which is why cat and Yorkie nips are so painful and so likely to pierce your skin when the little beasts bite.

| Animals PSI | | |
|---|---|---|
| | Domestic cat | 20-60 |
| | Adult human | 120 |
| *Domestic Dogs* | Kangal | 743 |
| | Mastiff | 556 |
| | Rottweiler | 328 |
| | African wild dog | 317 |
| | American bulldog | 305 |
| | Pit bull | 12 |
| *Wild animals* | Nile crocodile | 2,500-6000 |
| | Hippopotamus | 1,821 |
| | Wolf | 406 |
| | Great white shark | 60 |

respiratory infection, Patient A administered sulfa drugs and the horse recovered. But then the woman herself developed similar symptoms of respiratory infection and so did Patient B, her visiting seventy-one-year-old mother who had ridden, walked, and petted the horses. The younger woman recovered; her mother did not. Must you avoid horses? No. The solution is a solution: plenty of soap and water to wash your hands after working with a horse.[28]

## . . . to make friends with an elephant?

Dr. Seuss's "Horton" was right: "An elephant's faithful one hundred percent."[29] Iain Douglas-Hamilton, the zoologist who founded Save the Elephants in Nairobi, Kenya, remembers becoming so well acquainted with an elephant in Tanzania's Lake Manyara National Park early in his career that he could actually walk beside her in the wild. Douglas-Hamilton left the area in 1969 but when he came back four years later, the elephant "came right back up," and they went back to strolling through the park. So the next time someone says you have a memory like an elephant, take it as a compliment.[30]

## . . . to annoy an elephant?

No. In one dreadful moment in 2016, an elephant at Rabat Zoo in Morocco, picked up a rock in her trunk and hurled it, striking and killing a little girl taking pictures of the animals.[31] There was no obvious provocation, so there may never be an obvious explanation. But the simple fact is that when it comes to smarts, says Wildlife Conservation Society cognitive scientist Diana Reiss and colleagues at Emory University in Atlanta, elephants are right up there with dolphins, apes, and humans, an exclusive group of animals that can recognize their reflections in a mirror.[32] Perhaps the elephant mistook the girl or someone standing next to her for the person who once poked him (the elephant) with a stick.

### . . . to reach for a raccoon?

You protect your own pets with vaccination against rabies, but there's no practical way to control the incidence of rabies among wild animal populations where the disease is enzootic,[33] accounting for more than 90 percent of the reported cases in 2014. Raccoons are at the top of the list (30.2 percent of all animal cases during 2014), followed by bats (29.1 percent), skunks (26.3 percent), and foxes (5.2 percent).[34] Raccoons also harbor *Bayliscacaris procyonism* a.k.a. "raccoon roundworm," a parasite common in raccoon feces. If transferred to humans, the parasite may invade the lungs, liver, heart, eyes, and brain, and while recovery is possible, the sometimes fatal infection may leave survivors blind, in a coma, or with permanent brain damage. While the Centers for Disease Control and Prevention identified only seven cases between 2013 and 2015, the suspicion is that more may simply go unreported.[35]

### . . . to trifle with a spider?

One important marker in human evolution is the discovery and use of tools, including weapons. But we are not alone. Even insects use tools. Wasps use pebbles as hammers, and the Bolus spider (Mastophora cornigera) rolls its very own ball-like weapon, a blob of silk at the end of a long silk line similar to the boleadoras, a throwing weapon used by South American gauchos. "When an insect flies by, the spiders throw it; it attaches to the insect because it's sticky; and they reel them in," says Robert W. Schumaker, vice president of conservation and life sciences at the Indianapolis Zoo and author of the classic *Animal Tool Behavior*. Schumaker says the difference between us and the spider is that we think about making weapons while the insect acts from instinct and genetic programming.[36] While you are unlikely to be viewed as prey, stay clear lest the spider change her mind and toss some sticky stuff at you.

### . . . to swat a mosquito?

Yes. In 2015, the World Health Organization estimated there were 214 million cases of malaria among the 3.2 billion people living in parts of the world where the disease is endemic. Every year, about 1,500–2,000 cases turn up in the United States, almost always among people who've been traveling, who were infected abroad—and carried the problem home with them. These carriers may also infect any mosquito that bites them, thus sending out another messenger of malaria. In 2016, as Zika began to migrate around the world, the Centers for Disease Control and Prevention said the same thing could happen with this virus, which is transmitted by an infected *Aedes* species mosquito (*Ae. aegypti* and *Ae. albopictus*), the same insects that pass along the viruses that cause Dengue fever which some say is gets its name from the Swahili phrase *ka dinga pepo*, or "a disease caused by an evil spirit"[37] and *chikungunya*, meaning "to become contorted" in the Kimakonde language of Tanzania where the disease was first identified in 1972.[38]

### . . . to poke a hornet's nest?

Bad idea. If you are allergic to bee, wasp, or hornet stings, you know not to do this. If you are not allergic, your lifetime risk of dying from their sting is only about 1 in 64,706,[39] but poke that nest, and your risk of spending a very painful and unpleasant few hours or days is close to 100 percent.

# 2
# Food

"Part of the secret of success in life is to eat what you like and let the food fight it out inside."

—Mark Twain (1835-1910)

## Is it safe to drink the water?

Once upon a time, Americans worried about the water only when traveling to the far reaches of the earth, for example, Paris. To alleviate the problems due to unpleasant or unfamiliar bugs, travelers tossed some tetraglycine hydroperiodide (iodine) or NaDCC (chlorine)[40] tablets in with the extra underwear and, presto, change-o! Problem solved.[41] Today, as water quality around the world improves, there are still iffy places where protective tablets are a necessity. For Americans whose city infrastructure is so old that the water pipes contain lead, there is concern the lead may leak into the drinking water as happened famously in Flint, Michigan. On January 5, 2016, the

25

state and federal governments declared a state of emergency there, which eventually led to criminal charges against officials who had switched the source of the city's water supply without properly treating the pipes to prevent the lead contamination.[42]

## . . . to re-fill a water bottle?

That traveling bottle you clip on to your waistband? No problem. Just wash, rinse, dry, refill, and enjoy. But a disposable plastic bottle from the supermarket? Even the people who bottle and sell bottled water don't want you to refill that one. It's not because they want you to buy more. It's because "everyday wear and tear from repeated washings and reuse can lead to physical breakdown of the plastic, such as visible thinning or cracks. Bacteria can harbor in the cracks, posing a health risk. . . . and reuse of plastic water bottles can lead to bacterial contamination."[43] Washing gently by hand won't eliminate the problem, and dishwashers may create invisible cracks in disposable bottles in which bacteria may hide, says Scott Belcher, PhD and professor of pharmacology at the University of Cincinnati. He adds that heating the bottle "will certainly increase the rate at which chemicals can migrate from the plastic." As noted, non-disposable bottles can and should be safely cleaned. In 2002, researchers at the University of Calgary (Canada) took samples from non-disposable water bottles used by elementary school students and found more than six out of ten were contaminated with bacterial levels above those specified in safe drinking water rules and regulations. Best advice? Toss the disposable bottle, get yourself what Belcher recommends: A stainless steel or glass bottle with protective frames. "If you need a plastic bottle, I would recommend a polypropylene bottle, typically a white plastic . . . the types of non-reactive plastic bottles we often use in the lab." Wash after using. Let it dry completely inside and out. Now it's safe to refill.[44]

## . . . to eat snow?

It depends on where the snow fell and where it landed. Snow is just water that traveled through very cold air to solidify into flakes, and yes, it's true that no two of the gazillions falling around you are exactly alike. "It is extremely unlikely that two *complex* snowflakes will look *exactly* alike," says Caltech physicist Kenneth G. Libbrecht. "It's so extremely unlikely, in fact, that even if you looked at every one ever made you would not find any exact duplicates."[45] As for which ones are clean and safe, if the air through which the snowflakes traveled and the ground on which they landed are dirty, the snow will be as well. Here's a simple safety color code: If the snow is yellow, some person or animal probably peed on it. Red and green suggest algae. Black, brown, or gray say grit and grime, maybe from smokestacks or incinerators, or, in more exotic situations, an erupting volcano. But if the snow on top is clean, you can probably safely scoop that up, making sure not to collect any of the stuff underneath, next to the street or ground. And to be truly safe, chemistry expert Anne Marie Helmenstine, suggests melting the snow and running it through a coffee filter to remove any floating particles.[46]

## . . . to drink rainwater?

The same rules that govern eating or drinking snow apply to rain which, again, is simply water that runs through the air before it hits the ground. Obviously rainwater may pick up contaminants along the way, so you don't want to collect it in problematic locations, such as a place where there's been a radiation leak. But if you stand outside in a clean, clear open space and fill a clean glass with rain as it falls, you're likely fine. In 2009, the very first study of its kind, researchers at the Monash University Department of Epidemiology and Preventive Medicine (Australia) and Water Quality Research Australia gave water filters to three hundred families in Adelaide, the Australian city where most people get their water from rain-collecting tanks. The volunteers were then asked to keep records of their health over a one-year period. Nobody told the volunteers that half the "filters" really were filters while half were fakes, but it didn't matter. According to study leader Karin Leder, the results were the same for both groups with no measurable increase in gastro upset for those drinking the unfiltered water.[47] Of course, as with melted snow, you can improve rainwater's taste and quality by letting your glass sit for a while so that any sediment falls to the bottom, then pouring the water through a fine mesh strainer into a pot, boiling the water to kill off any bacteria, and, finally, running it through a paper coffee filter to eliminate pollen, mold, dust, insects, and assorted floating debris.

## . . . to leave canned food in an opened can?

The first cans often contained lead which could leach into the food. But in 1991, American food processors stopped using lead-soldered cans, and four years later the Food and Drug Administration ruled out the use of lead solder in all food cans, including those imported from other countries. Modern cans are made of steel and often lined with enamel or vinyl coating. Refrigerated food in an opened can is safe in its original container for a day or two. After that, natural spoilage may begin.

# Napoleon Bonaparte, Foodie Hero

An army moves on its stomach, so in-between trying to run France and ending up in exile on Elba, Napoleon Bonaparte had to feed his men. That was so difficult in the days before refrigeration that he offered a prize of twelve thousand French francs to anyone who could come up with a solution. In 1795, the winner was Nicholas Appert (1749–1841), a chef and part-time inventor who had spent the better part of two decades perfecting his method of packing meat and poultry in glass bottles, corking the bottles, sealing them with wax reinforced with wire, and then submerging the bottle in boiling water which halted bacterial growth and sterilized the food. How much was his prize worth? A lot. In 1800, one French franc equaled $20. Today, one US dollar from 1800 is equivalent to $18.81. Do the math:

**1 F (1800 AD) = $20**
**12,000 F (1800 AD) x $20 (1800 AD) = $240,000 US dollars (1800 AD)**
**1$ (1800 AD) = $18.81 (2017 AD)**
**$240,000 x $18.81 = $4,514,400 US dollars (2017 AD)**

Fifteen years after Appert claimed his prize, Britisher Peter Durance substituted metal containers for glass bottles.[48]

## . . . to drink hot coffee?

Extracting flavoring agents and other chemicals from coffee beans requires very hot water, so most restaurants brew theirs at temperatures ranging from 195°F to 205°F. Your own kitchen coffee maker is probably programmed to the same degree.[49] Serving, drinking, and enjoying this cup of delicious requires caution. As the consultants at Coffee Enterprises in Hinesburg, Vermont say, "Hot beverages are meant to be ingested in small sips, and anytime you spill a hot beverage on your skin, even at temperatures of 150°F, you will experience burning." Perhaps the most famous case of a coffee-spill burn Liebeck v. McDonald's Restaurants, the 1994 product liability lawsuit arising from a seventy-nine-year-old woman's suffering third-degree burns after accidentally spilling a cup of McDonald's hot coffee in her lap, leading to her being hospitalized for eight days for skin grafts and two years of medical

treatment.[50] You can argue, as many have, that it was a frivolous lawsuit, but the fact is that accidents happen. To be safe, let your cup cool before you lift it to your lips. If you get your coffee at a drive-through, make sure the lid on the cup is on tight, don't lift it to add sugar while you're driving, and never, ever hand the cup to a child in the car or at home.[51]

## . . . to drink cold brew coffee?

This hot new thing on the coffee market may not warm your heart. Back in the mid-90s, a number of European studies suggested that drinking even moderate amounts of coffee, say, five or six cups a day or less (no ounces specified) could send your cholesterol levels soaring. But the inevitable follow-up showed that it wasn't the coffee itself; it was the way you brewed it. In 2001, Michael J. Klag, the vice dean for clinical investigation at Johns Hopkins University School of Medicine in Baltimore examined a whole bunch of studies showing a relationship between coffee and cholesterol. He discovered that the culprit was unfiltered coffee—the kind you get when you make coffee in a "French" coffee press or an old-fashioned percolator, or when you boil ground coffee beans to make that thick, sweet Turkish coffee. Unfiltered coffee delivers large amounts of cafestol and kaweol, two members of a chemical family called diterpines that can raise your cholesterol.[52] Ditto for any cold brew coffee prepared by simply adding ground coffee beans to water and letting the mixture sit until the liquid turns brown. The simple solution is to pour the cold coffee through a filter to reduce or remove the offending chemicals—which are sometimes surprisingly protective: Both cafestol and kahweol appear to neutralize several known carcinogens, another scientific example of how you get to pick your poison.[53]

## . . . to switch to tea?

Atherosclerosis, a.k.a. "hardening of the arteries," happens when a mix of fats including cholesterol binds with cellular wastes, calcium, and the blood-clotting factor fibrin calcifies into a clump that may block the flow of blood through a blood vessel. Some studies show coffee may increase calcification. Others don't. The good news is tea. Data from the National Institutes of Health Multi-Ethnic Study of Atherosclerosis (MESA) suggests that drinking as little as one cup of black or green tea a day may slow or prevent calcification due to its protective antioxidants thearubigins, epi-catechins, and catechins. When Johns Hopkins researcher Elliot P. Miller and his colleague compared stats from 6,500 men and woman age 44 to 84 who filled out what-do-you-eat question-naires at six separate university health centers the tea drinkers had cleaner arteries. *Caveat emptor*: These are observational studies, so Miller says he can't say for sure it was the tea or just the healthier lifestyle of the tea drinkers.[54]

## . . . to drink tea to lose weight?

Americans aren't the only ones whose bodies are popping the buttons on their clothes. Obesity is a major problem around the world, so we've all heard about magic foods that will burn the fat right off our love handles. Most don't. Green tea may. In 2010, sci-entists at the Unilever R&D Shanghai Research Centre in Shang-hai assembled a group of 182 "moderately overweight" Chinese volunteers and divided them into four groups to see if the antiox-idant catechins in green tea could help them lose weight. Group #1 received two cups of regular green tea a day for ninety days (30 milligrams catechins, 10 milligrams caffeine). Group #2 received one serving of the regular and one serving of an extra high-catechin green tea (458 milligrams catechins, 104 milligrams caffeine). Group #3 received two servings of a high-catechin/high caffeine green tea (468 milligrams catechins, 126 milligrams caffeine/day). Group #4 received two servings of a super extra high-catechin green tea (886 milligrams catechins, 198 milligrams caffeine/day). At the end of ninety days, the people in Group #3 had lost about 2.2 inches in "intra-abdominal fat (IAF)," just under an inch in waist circumference and 2.6 pounds/1.2 kilograms body weight vs. 1/10th of a pound for those drinking regular green tea. In short, "consumption of two servings of an extra high-catechin GT leads to improvements in body composition and reduces abdominal fat-ness in moderately overweight Chinese subjects."[55] How the rest of the world's bodies react remains to be seen.

## . . . to eat powdered caffeine?

The Food and Drug Administration says a single teaspoon of the powder has as much caffeine as twenty-eight cups of brewed coffee and probably more cups of tea than you can count. Drink too much coffee or tea, and you're likely to vibrate. The powder with its concentrated stimulant may escalate that to caffeine overdose: vomiting, diarrhea, fast or erratic heartbeat, disorientation, seizures, and maybe death.[56]

## . . . to down an energy drink?

Literally dozens of reputable studies show that moderate amounts of caffeine improve athletic performance and endurance, but "energy drinks" and "energy shots" are not moderate products. The drinks (up to 24 ounces) and the shots (2 to 3 ounces) both deliver the same magic you get with caffeinated coffee or tea. The difference is that normal servings of coffee and tea have moderate amounts of caffeine while the "energy" beverages are packed to bursting. A really big 24-ounce drink may have up to 500 milligrams caffeine, about as much as you'd get from three 8-ounce or five 5-ounce cups of coffee, or more than ten times the amount of caffeine (47 milligrams) in an 8-ounce cup of brewed black tea.[57] A 2-ounce shot may contain up to 200 milligrams of caffeine, equal to two 5-ounce cups of coffee or three to four cups of tea. All that caffeine will certainly make you temporarily more alert, maybe even sufficiently alert to recognize the effects of caffeine overdose. (See previous entry.[58])

### . . . to sober up with an energy drink?

If you've had too much alcohol and are now chugging an energy drink to reverse the effects, forget it. All you will do it turn yourself into a "wide-awake drunk," meaning that the caffeine will mask alcohol's depressant effects, leaving you unable to recognize how intoxicated you are.[59]

### . . . to eat out (#1)?

In a restaurant, that is. The food's likely not as worrisome as the table and the menu. The rag used to wipe off the table top when you sit down has wiped down lots of surfaces before it got to you, a good reason to mind your mother and keep your elbows off the table. As for the menu, you may want to put on surgical gloves before picking it up. After all, who know how many hands have held it before it got to you? And who knows where those hands have been?[60]

### . . . to eat out (#2)?

Did you bring the baby with you? Did you ask for a high chair so he doesn't slide off the seat? Did you think about how many babies may have touched the chair or sneezed on it or (sorry about this) had a leaking diaper? Did you consider *Consumer Reports*' suggestion to bring your own portable chair next time?[61]

### . . . to eat out (#3)?

If we're talking family picnic—absent ants, flying insects, and an unexpected rain shower—it's likely to be safer than that restaurant because you chose and cooked the food, packed hot and cold items in the correctly insulated containers, and brought your own clean utensils. But if we're talking sidewalk cafes in big cities like New York, breathe carefully. Your "café" is likely to be a table set on a sidewalk bordered by a busy stream of noisy, maybe noxious, cars. Not the most pleasant place to lift a glass or bite into a burger.

## . . . to eat the salad (#1)?

Sometimes, yes. Sometimes, not so much. Salad greens grow close to the soil and are therefore easily contaminated. Once picked, they may pick up pathogens from other foods in a less-than-perfectly clean processing plant. Buying them packed in pretty plastic bags is no guarantee of safety. In 2013, the Food and Drug Administration issued more than twenty recalls for packaged salads, romaine lettuce, and spinach mostly due to the presence of listeria or *E. coli* bacteria. The possible solution? Wash, wash, wash your greens after digging up and before digging in.[62]

## . . . to eat the salad (#2)?

Moving past the clean food issue, consider the nutrition status of your salad. Toss the dish at home and you know exactly what's in the bowl and what it is worth nutrition-wise. Outside, it's another story. The website LiveStrong.com names the not-so-goods starting with Applebee's 1,340 calories, 2,630 milligrams sodium, 64 grams saturated fat and 64 grams sugar "Pecan Crusted Chicken Salad" designated one of the five worst American chain restaurant meals.[63] Take heart—and fewer calories, less fat, sodium, and sugar —with better choices, even at fast food emporia. For example, as this is written, these are the stats for McDonald's, Wendy's, and Burger King's best greenery nutrition bargains:

| McDonald's Bacon Ranch Grilled Chicken Salad | 320 calories & 14 grams fat[64] |
|---|---|
| Wendy's Summer Berry Chicken Salad | 380 calories & 9 grams fat [65] |
| Burger King's Garden Grilled Chicken Salad with Tendergrill (No Dressing) | 320 calories and 14 grams fat [66] |

Things may change, so check the menu.

### . . . to eat the salad (#3)?

Once upon a time, salad bars were salad bars, stocked with greens and fixings such as croutons and dressings. At that point, your main concern was whether the veggies were clean and how many calories were in the dressings. Today, as "salad bars" have expanded to included hot foods, cold foods, mixed grain dishes, and pre-mixed salads complete with mayonnaise, temperature

is all-important. Hot foods should be warm enough to give off steam. Cold foods should be cold enough to feel as though they have just come from (or are still in) a refrigerator. The edge of the counter should be pristine. There should be a plastic shield over the food that lets you see what's on the menu but keeps flies and germs and random floating hairs away. Otherwise, skip the bar and order elsewhere.[67]

### . . . to eat the salad (#4)?

Finally, speaking for the salad, over the years there have been rumors and testimonials, some more scientific than others, to the effect that plants respond to sound and touch. In a recent study, researchers at the University of Missouri's Division of Plant Sciences in the College of Agriculture, Food, and Natural

Resources and Bond Life Sciences Center put caterpillars on the leaves of rock grass plants, members of the *Brassicaceae* family that includes cabbage and mustard. As the little critters chomped away on the leaves, the scientists measured the way the plants moved in response to the vibrations. Then, ever mindful of the need for control groups, they set up two groups of rock grass plants, playing back recordings of these vibrations to the first but not the second. Then they put caterpillars on both sets of plants. Lo and behold, the greens that had been exposed to the caterpillar vibrations produced more mustard oils, a natural chemical in plants that caterpillars find unappealing. Even more remarkable, said study author Rex Cocroft, "plants exposed to different vibrations, including those made by a gentle wind or different insect sounds that share some acoustic features with caterpillar feeding vibrations did not increase their chemical defenses." That means plants can tell the difference between vibrations due to insects feeding and those due to other sources such as wind.[68] Maybe all that stuff about talking and singing to your begonias was right.

## . . . to eat spicy food?

Not if spicy foods upset your tummy, but if you've got a common cold, uncommonly spicy foods such as wasabi will make your mucous membranes leak so that your nose runs faster, hopefully washing out some congestive gunk. Spicy foods may also lengthen your life. A 2015 study of more than sixteen thousand American adults showed that after controlling for variables such as age, gender, smoking, cholesterol levels, and hypertension, people who regularly consumed hot red chili pepper were 13 percent less likely to die at an (undefined) early age.[69] This echoes an earlier study in China run by a spectacularly diverse group of scientists from Peking University, the Harvard School of Public Health, Brigham and Women's Hospital, Harvard Medical School, the University of Oxford, the Chinese Academy of

Medical Sciences, the Hainan Center for Disease Control and Prevention, the Gansu Center for Disease Control and Prevention, the Guangxi Center for Disease Control and Prevention, the Licang Center for Disease Control and Prevention, the Nangang Center for Disease Control and Prevention, and the China National Center for Food Safety Risk Assessment.[70] But the red pepper scientists did not know exactly how many red peppers the pepper people ate so they couldn't actually prove a cause-and-effect relationship. "The evidence isn't strong enough to make me change my diet," American co-author Benjamin Littenberg told *The New York Times*. "Don't smoke, limit calories, don't drink to excess, get a flu shot every year—those are things we have very convincing evidence will help you live longer. I don't know how much chili pepper to tell you to eat."[71]

## . . . to crunch a carrot?

You know that carrots protect your eyesight. Did you also know they can lend you a tan-like glow minus the skin cancer risk associated with radiation from the sun? Like tomatoes, the root veggies are a rich source of carotenoids, the class of naturally occurring, fat soluble antioxidant pigments called xanthins that includes alpha- and beta-carotene, beta-cryptoxanthin, lycopene, lutein, and zeaxanthin. These orange, red, and yellow chemicals travel from your gastrointestinal tract to your liver where they are partially transformed into a form of vitamin A (the vision nutrient). Then they swim through your blood stream to the rest of your body, including your skin. Excesses are eliminated in urine, sebum (the oily secretion from the sebaceous glands that waterproofs your skin), and sweat.[72] It's that last path—sweat—that may turn you golden. As a team of investigator led by Ian Stephen of the Universities of Bristol (UK) and St. Andrews (Scotland) confirmed in 2010, folks who feast on carotenoid-rich foods such as carrots and tomatoes really do end up with a more golden skin color. True, his subjects were all Caucasian, but Stephen suggests that that the golden effect may cross skin tones, although not as obviously.[73] Stephen's research confirms that there is nothing new under the sun or on sunny skin. On May 20, 1967, *The New Yorker Magazine*'s legendary medical writer Berton Rouche published an article called "The Orange Man," describing two patients who arrived at the University of Tennessee College of Medicine sporting bright orange skin. It turned out that both had been eating too many carrots and tomatoes. How much was too much? In one case, two cups of carrots plus two tomatoes a day.[74] The doctors suggested cutting back on the orange and red food. The patients complied. The orange faded away.

### . . . to drink orange juice?

The only thing more typically American than orange juice at breakfast is apple pie with any meal, any time at all. But when researchers at the University of Rochester Medical Center's Eastman Institute for Oral Health set out to learn if whitening products damage teeth, they got a big surprise. When it comes to denting dental enamel, the effects of whitening products pale compared to orange juice whose acidity is so strong that the tooth is literally washed away, decreasing the enamel hardness by as much as 84 percent, said Eastman's Yan Fang Ren. Conversely, no significant change in hardness or surface enamel were found from whitening. To reduce the damage while enjoying the juice or equally acidic sodas and "energy" drinks, swallow fast. The less time the liquid spends in your mouth, the lesser the damage.

### . . . to eat mushrooms?

The mushrooms on sale at your supermarket are safe and rich in B vitamins, including folate plus the mineral potassium. But about one hundred of the more than one thousand varieties of mushrooms are poisonous. In the United States, nearly nine of every ten cases of mushroom poisoning are due to just two of these species, the infamous *Amanita muscaria* and *Amanita phalloides*. To avoid possible death by fungi, unless you have an advanced degree in mushrooms, don't pick the ones you come across while walking in the woods.

## . . . to groove on magic mushrooms?

More than one hundred species of mushrooms are members of the genus *Psilocybin*, a.k.a. "magic mushrooms," whose distinguishing feature is the hallucinogen psilocybin. Although it has been illegal in the United States for decades, psilocybin (in mushrooms) has been a part of Native American and other cultures' spiritual experience since antiquity. Now modern medicine is investigating whether it may be useful in relieving depression, specifically in cancer patients. In 2016, *The New York Times* reported that a number of studies have shown "promising results" with about 80 percent of the patients given psilocybin exhibiting "clinically significant reductions in both psychological disorders, a response sustained some seven months after the single dose. Side effects were minimal." As is true of many psychotropic meds, nobody knows exactly how or why this happens although it seems that hallucinogens may behave like selective serotonin reuptake inhibitors (SSRIs) such as paroxetine/Paxil®, short-circuiting the inward thinking characteristic of depression. And, no, you should not rush out to the, um, dispenser on your corner for some psilocybin. The psilocybin patients were closely monitored and given supportive "talk therapy" to increase their sense of well-being.[75]

## . . . to binge on protein?

Protein is good for every body. It builds every cell, from bones to blood, repairs injured tissue, makes enzymes and hormones, and generally keeps you in tip-top shape. But you don't store the protein you consume, so you need a new supply every day. In 2005, the National Academy of Sciences Food and Nutrition Board set the recommended daily intake at 46 grams a day for a healthy adult woman and 56 grams a day for a healthy adult man. In places where there is an adequate supply of food, it is easy to meet these requirements with two to three 3-ounce servings of lean meat, fish, or poultry (21 grams each). Vegetarians can fill their quota with two eggs (12–16 grams), two slices of packaged fat-free cheese (10 grams), four slices of bread (3 grams each), and one cup of yogurt (10 grams). Vegans who do not eat any foods from animals, including dairy products, can do well with one cup of oatmeal (6 grams), one cup of soymilk (7 grams), 2 tablespoons peanut butter (8 grams), one to two slices of bread plus 6 ounces soy milk yogurt (6 grams), 6 ounces tofu (13 grams), one cup cooked brown rice (5 grams), and one cup steamed broccoli (5 grams). Protein requirements rise during pregnancy so pregnant women can build new tissue for themselves and their developing fetuses. Professional athletes and people who've been injured may also need extra protein to repair damaged tissue. Is it possible to overdose on something this healthful? Maybe. Newly popular products such as protein drinks and powders were developed originally for the elderly and those suffering from malnutrition. As a result they serve up proteins in amounts that far exceed the Academy's recommendations for healthy people. For example, one canned protein drink may contain almost as much protein as an 8-ounce steak. It's true that high protein diets have been touted for fast weight loss, but they may also increase the risk of kidney problems and, theoretically, because protein increases cell multiplication, may contribute to cancer later in life. In 2014, researchers at the University of Southern California's Longevity Institute found that adults who consumed large amounts of protein between ages fifty and sixty-five were four times more likely than those who ate less protein to die of cancer. Clearly, that's a study begging for follow-up.[76]

## . . . to satisfy your sweet tooth?

You mean, will eating sugar kill you? It's complicated. Most of us think of "sugar" as that white stuff we use to sweeten our coffee. Nutritionists, on the other hand, define sugars as the building blocks of carbohydrates, similar to amino acids as the building blocks of proteins. Carbs come in two basic versions: simple and complex, based on the number of sugar units they comprise. A simple carb (monosaccharide, from the Greek words *monos* meaning "single" and *sakharos* meaning "sugar") is made of only one kind of sugar unit. Glucose ("blood sugar") and fructose ("fruit sugar") are monosaccharides. A disaccharide is a complex carbohydrate built of two kinds of sugar units. The best known disaccharide is sucrose (table sugar) which is made of units of glucose and fructose. Another common disaccharide, lactose, the natural sugar in milk, is made of glucose and galactose. Finally, a polysaccharide is a complex carbohydrate whose molecules have anywhere from three to several thousand units of sugar. Each molecule of raffinose, a complex carb found in veggies, has one unit each of galactose, glucose, and fructose. Stachyose, also found in vegetables, has one glucose unit, one fructose, and two galactose units. Molecules of starches, the carbs in grains, may have many thousands of glucose units stuck together in a long chain.

Despite their different molecule make-up, every sugar you put into your mouth sends a signal to your pancreas to release insulin, the hormone that enables you to break carbs apart and tells your cells to begin grabbing nutrients from your bloodstream so you can get the glucose—the fuel on which your body runs.[77] Monosaccharides trigger a quicker and higher insulin response than do complex carbs, sending more sugar directly into your blood stream. If your body secretes more insulin than you need to convert the carbs, the cells simply shut down their pickup, a phenomenon known as insulin resistance that allows glucose and fatty acids including cholesterol to pile up in your blood. This may lead to hyperinsulinemia which may lead to Type 2 diabetes, not to men-

## What's in a name?
## Added Sugars in Your Food[79]

There are more than fifty different names for the different kinds of added sugar, all of which may legally make their way on to the label's ingredient list. Of course, to paraphrase Good Will Shakespeare, "That which we call sugar, by any other name will taste as sweet."

| | |
|---|---|
| Agave nectar | Glucose |
| Brown sugar | High fructose corn syrup |
| Cane crystals | Honey syrup |
| Cane sugar | Invert sugar |
| Corn sweetener | Maltose |
| Corn syrup | Malt syrup |
| Crystalline fructose | Maple sugar |
| Dextrose | Molasses |
| Evaporated cane juice | Raw sugar |
| Fructose | Sucrose |
| Fruit juice concentrate | |

tion a higher risk of heart disease, obesity, and a host of other endocrine disorders, most of which may be avoided by following the golden rule propounded by the ancient Greeks, "Everything in moderation."

## . . . to eat foods with added sugar?

The sweet sugars in your food fall into two categories: natural and added. As their name implies, the former occur naturally in foods; the latter are what food processors toss into all kinds of products from breakfast cereals to those handy little plastic cups of fruit cocktail. On May 20, 2016, the Food and Drug Administration added "added sugars," in grams and as percent Daily Value (%DV), to the nutrition facts label on your food.[78]

## . . . to eat foods with high-fructose corn syrup?

High fructose corn syrup (HFCS), a.k.a. glucose-fructose, is made by processing corn starch into a syrup and converting some of its glucose into fructose. As it has become a more common ingredient in sodas and other products, Americans have gotten fatter. *Post hoc, propter hoc*, some believe the first (obesity) is due to the second (HFCS). Not everyone has joined the parade because plain and simple science shows that the syrup is chemically similar to table sugar. True, there is a question as to whether the human body handles the syrup differently than the sandy solid. But as Katherine Zeratsky, a registered dietician at the Mayo Clinic, says, right now there is simply not sufficient proof that the syrup is any less healthy than other sweeteners.[80]

## . . . to drink diet sodas #1?

Diet sodas replace table sugar with artificial sweeteners some people consider iffy on nutritional health. For example, aspartame (NutraSweet®, Equal®) appears to raise a lab rat's risk of "metabolic syndrome," the group of nasties that includes high blood pressure, higher cholesterol levels and, yes, a bigger but not necessarily better body perhaps by preventing the enzyme intestinal alkaline phosphatase (IAP) from breaking down fats during digestion. This may or may not happen in human beings, but for the time being Dr. Richard Hodin, senior author of the Massachusetts General Hospital/Harvard Medical School study, wants you to know that water is a better alternative than diet soda.[81]

### . . . to drink diet sodas #2?

More than one hundred studies over more than twenty years have shown that sucralose, the artificial sweetener in Splenda® found in many diet sodas is not a carcinogen. Then, out of the blue, a study at the Ramazzini Institute in Bologna (Italy) said, "Oops, maybe we were wrong." The Italian researchers fed 843 mice varying doses of sucralose from the time they were fetuses until their natural deaths after which post-mortem examinations showed that the more sucralose the mice got throughout their lives, the more likely they were to develop leukemia. The sucralose diet also seemed to interfere with the animals' absorption of medical drugs. Obviously, this study demands a follow-up to replicate the results and figure out if they are important for human beings. As of 2015, this had not yet happened.[82]

### . . . to eat ice cream?

If you can manage to control your portions, enjoy. Especially at breakfast. In one of those inventive experiments scientists love, Yoshihiko Koga ran a series of clinical trials at Tokyo's Kyorin University in which one group of volunteers were given ice cream right after they opened their eyes in the morning; a second group did not. Then, Koga put both the ice cream people and their sweets-deprived confreres through a series of mental exercises on a computer. The result? Those who got the ice cream reacted faster and were able to process information better than those who didn't. The ice cream people also demonstrated an increase in high-frequency alpha waves, electrical activity in the brain believed to play a role in coordinating communication between brain cells which leads to higher levels of alertness. To make sure that these reactions weren't due simply to the volunteers' brains being shocked awake by exposure to the cold ice cream, Koga re-ran his experiment, this time with cold water. That also produced a more alert brain but not as alert as the one belonging to people who ate ice cream. Exactly what's going on here remains to be proven, but there's also been a study showing that eating chocolate cake for breakfast helps you lose—yes, lose—weight.[83]

## . . . to salt your food?

Sodium is an electrolyte, one of a trio that includes potassium and chloride. The three chemicals dissolve in water, separating into particles called ions that conduct electricity, enabling your cells to transmit messages back and forth. The Food and Nutrition Board of the Institute of Medicine's National Academy of Sciences sets the recommended daily Adequate Intake (AI) of sodium for an adult age eighteen to fifty at 1,500 milligrams, slightly less than a teaspoon. For people whose bodies are more than normally sensitive to sodium, consuming more than that may trigger hypertension (high blood pressure) which is usually alleviated by reducing salt intake. Others, however, seem to be able to consume salt by the barrel without experiencing any ill effects. That being true, several studies suggest that as a general rule the problem with sodium lies at the opposite ends of the salty spectrum. For example, in 2011, a report from a multi-nation study that followed nearly four thousand people in Belgium, Poland, the Czech Republic, and the Russian Federation for almost ten years showed that those most likely to develop sodium-linked cardiovascular disease or high blood pressure were, respectively, the people who consumed very little salt and those who consumed a lot.[84] Conclusion? One shake of the salt cellar, fine; two shakes, iffy, three shakes, maybe not.

### . . . to drink alcohol?

"Moderate" drinking—two a day for a man, one for a woman[85] —relaxes your muscles, lightens your mood, and lowers your risk of cardiovascular disease in three specific ways. First, the alcohol reduces the stickiness of blood platelets (small particles that can clump together to form an artery-blocking blood clot). Second, alcohol relaxes and temporarily expands your blood vessels. Third, it increases the amount of HDLs ("good cholesterol" in your blood. While red wine gets most of the applause, all alcohol beverages—wine, beer, spirits—produce the beneficial effects. And here's an extra added and often overlooked and unmentioned benefit: Moderate drinking may even keep your brain active and vital as you grow older. The title of this study says it all: "Moderate alcohol consumption in older adults is associated with better cognition and well-being than abstinence."[86] That's one more good reason to say "To your health" when lifting a glass.

### . . . to mix your drinks?

Is drinking wine and distilled spirits such as whisky, gin, or vodka within gulping distance of each other more harmful than guzzling either one alone? No. Every alcoholic beverage is alcohol plus water; wine and beer also contain some residue of the foods from which they were made. The term ABV on the can, bottle, or box label measures the alcohol content as a percentage of all the liquid in the container. For example, if your container holds 10 ounces of liquid and 1 ounce of that is alcohol, the product is 10 percent ABV, the alcohol content divided by the total amount of liquid. Proof, an older term to describe alcohol content, is two times the ABV. For example, an alcohol beverage that is 10 percent alcohol by volume

## This Drink Equals That Drink

How will how much alcohol affect you? What matters isn't what beverage is in your glass, it's how much alcohol is in the beverage. That varies by type, but to make it easier for you to estimate your intake, the National Institute of Alcohol Abuse and Alcoholism (NIAAA) presents this handy equivalence table:

**12 fluid ounces of regular beer (about 5% alcohol) =**
**8 to 9 fluid ounces of malt liquor (about 7 % alcohol) =**
**5 fluid ounces of table wine (about 12 % alcohol) =**
**1.5 fluid ounce shot of 80-proof distilled spirits (about 40 % alcohol)[88]**

is 20 proof.[87] The more alcohol you drink, the more you will experience its effects ranging from inebriation now to a headache, tummy ache, muscle aches, and a really serious thirst tomorrow morning.

### . . . to drink and drive?

No.

### . . . to eat and drink while pregnant?

You're right. That headline is just a tease. Of course, a pregnant woman needs a healthful diet to nurture both herself and her growing fetus. But the list of potential hazards includes a lot of otherwise healthful food and beverages. For example, virtually all hard cheeses such as cheddar or Swiss cheese are safe, but soft cheeses such as queso blanco or fromage blanc are made from unpasteurized milk and thus more likely to harbor listeria bacteria which can cause miscarriage, fetal illness, or fetal death even if you don't feel sick yourself. And yes, that's true as well of unpasteurized milk.[89] Some cured meat such as Parma ham or fresh pate may also harbor *Salmonella*. Liver is a risky treat because it's very high in retinol (natural vitamin A) which—in large amounts—may trigger birth defects in the fetus. And then there's fish. The Food and Drug Administration says wild salmon, scallops, shrimp (most wild and United States farmed), tilapia, catfish, crab, trout, flounder, and sole (flatfish) are safely low in mercury, but shark, swordfish, king mackerel, and tilefish may contain unsafe levels that may damage a developing fetal brain as well as cause vision and hearing problems.[90] Tuna raises questions. In 2004, the Food and Drug Administration urged women and young children to eat no more than 12 ounces of a variety of fish and shellfish with lower levels of mercury (including canned light tuna) or 6 ounces of white tuna (albacore) per week to minimize mercury risks. Ten years later, *Consumer Reports* urged all pregnant women to avoid tuna entirely. As for liquid refreshment, some say avoid alcohol entirely, others say one or two drinks a week is fine. Drinking lots of caffeine on a regular basis in pregnancy has been linked to miscarriage and low-birth weight infants; the prudent suggestion is to cut back on caffeine to maybe 200 milligrams a day.[91] Caffeine content varies by brand of coffee, but an average 8-ounce cup of brewed regular coffee has from 95–200 milligrams caffeine; a 1-ounce regular restaurant espresso, 47–75 milligrams; an 8-ounce cup of black tea, 14–75 milligrams (green tea, slightly less); a 12-ounce can of regular soda, up to 39 milligrams; a 12-ounce can of caffeine-free soda, 0.

### . . . to eat Albacore tuna?

Albacore tuna is prettier and thus generally more expensive than light tuna.[92] Better yet, 3.5 ounces/100 grams samples of drained, water-pack white tuna generally have more heart healthy Omega 3 fatty acids. On the other hand, an equal amount of light

### Etymology factoid

The name "albacore" looks like it might mean white ("alba"), but it actually comes from the "Portuguese *alba-cora*, from Arabic *al bakara* 'milk cow;' the fish so called for its size"[94] which can be truly impressive. The Atlantic blue fin tuna may grow as long as 15 feet and reach 1,500 pounds in weight.[95]

tuna has about 15 percent fewer calories, 14 percent less cholesterol, more iron and B vitamins, and less mercury. When *Consumer Reports* tested the tunas, they found, on average, 0.217 to 0.774 ppm (parts per million) mercury in the white tuna sample and 0.018 to 0.176 ppm in the light. Which means that if you eat 5 ounces of either white or light tuna, you will exceed recommended guidelines, but the light tuna exceeds them by less.[93]

### . . . to eat off the floor?

You know that mythical housewife whose home is so clean you can eat off the floor? Turns out, she isn't doing her family any good because the "five-second rule"—it's safe to eat food you've dropped on the floor so long as you pick it up five seconds after it hits the ground—is equally mythical. To prove the point, Rutgers University microbiologist Donald Schaffner dropped chunks of watermelon, pieces of bread, pieces of bread with butter, and gummy candies on four different surfaces: stainless steel, ceramic tile, wood, and carpet. Then he picked each one up after less than one second down, five seconds, thirty seconds, and even three hundred seconds (that's five minutes) and counted the bacteria on the food. Watermelon, which is wet, accumulated the highest number of bugs and litter; gummy candy, the least. Carpet transferred less detritus than did smooth stainless steel. But all the food samples teemed with tiny critters, even after just a one second touchdown.[96] Of course there's a contrarian in the kitchen. "I'm a Doctor," Indiana University pediatrician Aaron Carroll wrote in *The New York Times*, "and if I drop food on the kitchen floor, I still eat it." Carroll's position is simple: Bacteria are everywhere and some of the things we touch everyday are far more contaminated than the kitchen floor. As proof, he cites one 1998 study showing that your floor has about three colonies of coliform bacteria[97] per square inch. While that sounds scary, the refrigerator door handle had 5.37; the kitchen counter, 5.75; the bathroom faucet handle, 15.84; the flush handle on the toilet, 34.65; and the sponge sitting on the kitchen sink a mind-blowing 20,000,000. "Things get dirty when lots of hands touch them," Carroll says. "The alternative is to realize that for most of us, our immune systems are pretty hardy. We've all been touching this dirty stuff for a long time, without knowing it, and doing just fine."[98]

### . . . to eat at bedtime?

Acid reflux ("heartburn") is what happens when acidic digestive juices flow up and back from your stomach into your esophagus. More than sixty million American adults experience this at least once a month; at least twenty-five million, once a day. Sitting up while eating and remaining upright for a few hours afterwards allows your stomach to empty significantly, reducing the risk of backward flow. Eating while lying down—the normal position when you are getting ready to go to sleep—makes reflux more likely.[99] The better way: no food within three hours of bedtime.[100]

### . . . to eat a coconut?

Coconut oil is high in saturated fats, but coconut "milk" (the thin fluid extracted from coconut meat) isn't, so even the American Heart Association, which warns us off the oil, offers recipes made with the "milk." But the true coconut hazard isn't eating coconut oil or milk or high fiber coconut meat. It's sitting under a coconut tree. The apple that fell on Isaac Newton's head in 1666 triggered his understanding of gravity. A coconut falling on yours might frazzle your brain because, as the National Center for Biotechnology Information explains, the blow delivered by a 9-pound coconut falling from a 100-foot tree can deliver more than the force of 1 metric ton (2204.62262 pounds).[101] Death by falling coconut is not a common occurrence, but it has happened. For example, on January 17, 1995, a seventy-six-year-old coconut-picker in Kota Baru (Malaysia) was killed when the monkey he employed to gather coconuts from trees hurled one that split open his owner's skull.[102] In short, if you must sit under a coconut tree, don't annoy the monkeys.

### . . . to eat licorice?

Licorice root (scientific name glycyrrhiza) has a long and honorable history in herbal medicine, both Eastern and Western, primarily to treat gastric upset, sooth a sore throat, and calm a cough. But no remedy, "natural" or otherwise, is completely free of adverse effects. The natural sweetener in licorice root is glycyrrhizin.[103] Candy makers mix it with sugar and a "binder," most commonly flour plus gum plus gelatin, and maybe beeswax to make it shine and molasses for the rich dark color licorice lovers like. As a supplement or in candy, large amounts of glycyrrhizin may lower potassium levels, maybe leading to an abnormal heartbeat and exacerbating hypertension, particularly in people older than forty with a history of heart disease or high blood pressure. (Potassium levels usually go back to normal when consumption of black licorice stops.) Equally worrisome is a Finnish study showing that pregnant women who consume high amounts of glycyrrhizin may be more likely to deliver prematurely.[104] How do you enjoy licorice without side effects? The confectioner's secret is that many "licorice" or "licorice flavor" candies made and sold in the United States are flavored with anise oil which tastes and smells like licorice rather than glycyrrhizin. As for dietary supplements, it pays to read the label. Some "licorice root" sold in health food stores may actually be DGL or "deglycyrrhizinated licorice." Or you could just switch colors: Red licorice rarely contains licorice extract, relying instead on natural or artificial cherry or strawberry flavoring.

# 3

# Health

"Early to bed and early to rise
makes a man healthy, wealthy and wise."

—Benjamin Franklin (1706-1790)

### Is it safe to blow your nose?

In 2009, infectious disease experts at the University of Virginia ran CT scans to see what happens inside the nasal sinuses[105] when a human coughs, sneezes, or blows his or her nose. Nothing interesting occurred when volunteers coughed or sneezed, but blowing both nostrils at once created pressure strong enough to send mucus from the nostrils back into the sinuses. Is letting your nose drip the only alternative? No. As otolaryngologist Anil Kumar Lawani of New York Presbyterian Hospital told *The New York Times*, it may help to take a decongestant that temporarily dries your nasal passages. And if you must blow, you can lower the blowback pressure by blowing just one nostril at a time.[106]

### . . . to cover a sneeze with your hand?

If you do this when you have a cold, yes, you will spray viruses on your hand. That's icky, but the good news is that they can't re-infect you. There are literally hundreds of viruses known to cause the not-so-common cold. Once you've had one of them, such as the one caused by the viruses you just sneezed onto your hand, you're immune to that one although not necessarily to the one the person next to you sneezed out. Absent a tissue, it seems common courtesy to cover your sneeze to avoid spraying someone else. And remember: unless you wash your hand right away, you will contaminate the next thing or place you touch, spreading your particular bug to anyone who touches whatever you've just contaminated.[107]

### . . . to sneeze around your dog?

Got the flu? Scientists at the University of Rochester School of Medicine and Dentistry want you to know that not only can your puppy catch what you've got, he's a "mixing vessel" whose body might possibly produce new flu strains to bounce right back at you. To reduce the risk, when you get your shot, you may soon be able to give him his. A team from the Veterinary Medicine at Cornell University and the University of Glasgow Centre for Virus Research plans to test flu vaccines in clinical trials with dogs, a commendable sort of animal research because it benefits animals as well as humans.[108]

### . . . to open your eyes when you sneeze?

It's safe, but it's really hard to do. A sneeze is an involuntary reaction that occurs when something irritates the tissue inside your nose, sending a signal to your trigeminal nerve—the large one responsible for facial sensation and motor functions such as chewing. The trigeminal then alerts your medulla oblongata, the part of your brain that controls involuntary reaction such as sneezing. Your medulla oblongata tells your chest to expand, filling your lungs with air which you expel when you sneeze. Why do you shut your eyes? Nobody knows. It appears to be just a reflex similar to how your leg jumps when your doctor taps your knee.

### . . . to stare at a bright light?

Some people sneeze whenever they look into a very bright light. Scientists call this the ACHOO (autosomal dominant compelling helio-ophthalmic outburst) syndrome. It seems to be a genetic trait identified as early as 1951 and confirmed in a 2016 report from the Complejo Hospitalario de Pontevedra in Spain where it was linked to the presence of prominent corneal nerves. But there were only twelve people in the sample, all members of the same family, eight of whom sneezed at the light. Sensibly, the Pontevedra researchers say more studies with more people are needed.[109]

### . . . to kiss a human?

This is not a frivolous question. Kissing isn't just for fun; it also reduces stress and enhances emotional bonds between the participants.[110] There are two types of kissing, "light" and "deep."[111] The former means kissing with your mouth closed; the latter, a.k.a. "French kissing," with your mouth open. Naturally, either embrace implies intimate contact with another human being, and kissing with your mouth open allows the exchange of saliva, thus facilitating the transmission of a whole list of all sorts of things you'd rather avoid—such as the bacteria that cause tooth decay and syphilis, as well as the viruses responsible for colds, flu, herpes, oral warts, hepatitis B, and AIDS. Obviously, none of these possibilities has ever had even the tiniest effect on the continuing human desire to kiss open-mouthed.

## You could look it up

There are thirty-six pages of "kiss" books on Amazon.com ranging from the celebrity semi-sociological *The Book of Kisses* (Diane Publishing Company, 1993) to the pragmatic *How to Be a Good Kisser: Your Guide to Becoming a Good Kisser (How to Make Out + Other French Kissing Tips)* (CreateSpace Independent Publishing Platform, 2015) and the seriously how-to-succeed *Kiss, Bow, or Shake Hands: How to Do Business in Sixty Countries* (Adams Media, 2006), plus two entries in *Wikipedia* ("Kiss" and "French Kiss"), one in *WikiHow* "How to Kiss with pictures," one in the *Encyclopedia Britannica*, and as of this writing at least six on *WebMd.com* ("What's So Great About Kissing?," "Kissing Secrets Revealed," "Quiz: Kiss and Tell: What Do You Know About Locking Lips?," "Pucker Up! How to Be a Better Kisser," "When a Kiss Is More Than Just a Kiss," and, of course, the ever popular, "Q. Is it possible to get an STD from kissing?"

### . . . to shake your doctor's hand?

Mark S. Sklansky, chief of the Division of Pediatric Cardiology at the David Geffen School of Medicine at UCLA, knows that the handshake is a time-honored gesture of respect and trust, and that when shared by doctor and patient, it has the power to "comfort and to calm." But his research tells him that given the wide contacts of healthcare workers in hospitals and in a doctor's office "cross-contamination of health care workers' hands commonly occurs through routine patient and environmental contact." Hands, he says, are "far dirtier than most of the rest of the body! So, practically speaking, one can either insist upon proper hand hygiene before and after handshaking, or simply forego the handshake." How about a simple bow instead?[112]

## . . . to shake your nurse's hand?

Sorry: No studies on this one. Either nurses simply have cleaner hands than doctors or, more likely, no one thought to test them.

## . . . to clean your ears?

Earwax, a.k.a. cerumen from the Latin word *cera* meaning "wax," comprises oils secreted by glands inside your ear canal to help to keep the inside of your ear clean by trapping dust and dirt and maybe even a teensy passing bug. Different people produce different kinds of earwax. For example, the wax in European and African ears is usually stickier than that in ears from northeastern Asia. As we get older, everyone's ears produce more wax but at any age an individual can make too much earwax, blocking the ear and interfering with hearing. How to remove it? As the people at the American Speech Language and Learning Association remind us, "Put nothing smaller than your elbow in your ear." Using sharpies such as toothpicks to scrape away the wax might puncture your eardrum. Even a cotton-ended Q-tip® could be less than healthful; push too hard and you may shove the wax further into your ear. Ordinarily, the wax will work its way out itself, but if it doesn't and you don't seem to hear as well as you usually do, your best bet is an audiologist who can do the job quickly and safely.[113]

## . . . to fast?

Different people define fasting differently. Some say it is a minimum amount of food, perhaps one apple and one pear a day, plus water. Others say it's no food, but plenty of water. A third group says the first two are wimps: For them, a fast is no food, no water, no kidding. In all three types of fasts, the same physiological rules apply. At first, for about three days without food, you live off the glucose ("blood sugar") still circulating through your system. After that, your body begins to extract stored energy from body fat. When that's depleted, you move on to digesting your muscles (including your heart) and other vital organs. How long after that will you live? Obviously, no decent society would sanction a controlled study to pinpoint the exact time from your last meal to your last breath, but survival after months or even years of near-total starvation has often occurred historically during periods of famine and most notoriously in German concentration camps during World War II. Well-documented studies show that political hunger strikers have lived for as long as seven weeks without food or water; the body carefully moderates its metabolism, slowing basic functions such as heartbeat and respiration to cope with a reduced supply of energy. In medical situations, doctors may encounter voluntary starvation in patients suffering from eating disorders such as anorexia nervosa and bulimia where death due to organ failure is likely when the patient's weight drops to 80 pounds or less and the BMI (body mass index), normally 18 to 24, falls to 12.5 or 12. But much depends on your age, your weight, your genes, and your health when the fast begins and of course, how much food actually passes your lips. Individual survival time varies markedly.[114]

## Famous Fasters

Deuteronomy 9:9-18 says Moses fasted for forty days before ascending the mountain to receive the Ten Commandments.

Esther fasted for three days before asking King Ahasuerus to save the Jews from Haman. Ahasuerus said, okay, and hanged Haman and his sons, thus giving birth to the holiday of Purim as recounted in Esther 4:15-17.

Mohandas Gandhi was a serial faster, first for three days in 1924 to reconcile warring factions of Hindus and Muslims, then six days in 1932 to bring the "untouchables" into Indian society, and finally three weeks in 1933 to "purify" himself.

British suffragette Marion Wallace Dunlop, jailed in July 1909 for tossing rocks at the windows of 10 Downing Street, fasted for ninety-one hours leading to the Prisoner's Temporary Discharge of Ill Health Act allowing hunger strikes and discharging sick inmates to recuperate and then return to finish their sentences.[115] Across the Pond, American suffragette Alice Paul fasted in 1917 at Virginia's Occoquan Workhouse and was sent to the psych ward to be force-fed raw eggs. After that, in both cases, in both countries, within a decade, women won the right to vote. The Nineteenth Amendment to the US Constitution was adopted in 1920; the British passed the Representation of the People (Equal Franchise) Act in 1928.

IRA members Thomas Ashe, Terence McSwiney, Denny Barry, and Bobby Sands fasted in 1917, 1917, 1922, and 1981, respectively, to protest British rule of Northern Ireland and conditions in British jails. Ashe and McSwiney died after being force-fed; Barry died after thirty-five days without food and water, and Sands, after sixty-six days.

Cesar Chavez fasted three times to highlight the difficulties facing American farm workers and their children, first for twenty-five days in 1968, then for twenty-five days in 1972, and finally for thirty-six days in 1988.[116]

Tiananmen students fasted for six days in The Square, beginning on May 13, 1989 and ending on May 19 when the Chinese government declared martial law.[117]

Mia Farrow, American actress, fasted for twelve days in 2009 to protest conditions in Darfur. When her doctor put an end to the fast, she passed the protest on to Virgin Airlines founder Richard Branson who fasted for three days.[118]

## . . . to limit liquids (#1)?

The average body of an average adult human is about 50-65 percent water.[119] Your lungs are about 98 percent water; blood more than 80 percent; and the brain, about 70 percent. There is less water in fat than in muscle, so the male body (which has less body fat than does the female) is about 60 percent water vs. about 55 percent for the female. Regardless of gender, an overweight body has less water than a lean one.[120] Every day, the average human adult body perspires away about two cups of water, breathes away about a cup, and urinates away about six cups.[121] That adds up to, yes, more than eight cups, the long-standing recommendation for daily drinking. But long-standing doesn't mean "forever," and recent research suggests that because we get water in what we eat and drink, simply drinking when thirsty works just fine.[122]

## . . . to limit liquids (#2)?

Salty foods retain water in your body, so it's true that your weight may go up and down a pound or two from day to day depending on how much salt you eat. But trying to slim down by limiting liquids after downing, say, a bag of potato chips, is a very bad idea whose results may end up mirroring what happens to people who can't get any liquids at all. Lose a little water, and you'll be thirsty. Lose a little more without replacing it, and your circulation will slow as water seeps out of your blood cells, making you feel somewhat of out of sorts. Keep losing water without replacing it and nausea's next, along with skin flushes, tingling in your hands and feet, and quickened breathing and heartbeat. When your water deficit rises to about 10 percent of your body weight, your tongue swells, your kidneys start to fail, and our muscles clench in spasm. Next up or down, your vision and hearing sink, your tongue and skin shrink, and at a 20 percent loss without replacement, everything crashes.[123]

## . . . to drink a lot of water?

While dieters sometimes drink too little, athletes sometimes drink too much. It's true that you lose water when you perspire heavily while exercising. It's also true that you need to replace the liquid, but pouring too much water down your gullet may dilute the sodium your body. Because sodium maintains the liquid balance in your cells, diluting it may lead to hyponatremia, a.k.a. "water intoxication," a potentially fatal condition in which your cells and tissues retain too much liquid, causing them to swell. The mathematically inclined among you may wish to use the American College of Sports Medicine (ACSM) number to calculate exactly how much liquid you need to replace while working

out. Here's how: Step on a scale before exercising, checking your weight, then stepping back on the sale after a one hour workout and drinking 16 ounces to replace every pound lost during the workout hour. One pound lost; 16 ounces to drink. One half pound, 8 ounces. Or, just drink when you're thirsty.[124]

## . . . to drink lots of water to ameliorate a urinary infection?

Like the ACSM, researchers at Kings College Hospital in London think that drinking when thirsty is sensible advice, in this case for people suffering from a urinary tract infection who are commonly told to drink up as often as possible. The problem with the drink-as-much-as-possible regimen, the researchers say, is that the infection may cause your kidneys to work less efficiently and excrete less liquid, allowing water to fill up (flood?) in your body with unpleasant results (see above). They conclude we need more studies on this topic in order to come to an accurate conclusion.[125]

### . . . to drink your urine?

So there you are, in the middle of the Mojave Desert, miles from Las Vegas to the east and Los Angeles to the west. The sun is shining, the air is dry, you are really, really thirsty, but there's not a drop of water left in your canteen. Given the emergency, you can safely drink your urine, right? Not so fast. "Doctors have been trained to believe that urine is germ-free," said Linda Brubaker, MD of the Loyola University Chicago Strich School of Medicine, but that's a myth. In June 2014, Brubaker told the attendees at the 114th General Meeting of the American Society for Microbiology in Boston that her study of ninety women (no men) shows that even urine from healthy females carries bacteria, some potentially harmful, some not. Solution (no pun intended)? But there in the Mojave, it's an emergency. You might as well drink and if necessary take your medicine later. In Las Vegas. Or Los Angeles.[126]

### . . . to "hold it in"?

"Go Ask Alice!" is a site run by a team of Columbia University health specialists who answer all sorts of health questions, including the issue of whether, as one curious writer put it, "people can die from not going pee."

"Dear Reader," Alice answered, "put your fears to rest about dying from not using the toilet—it is extremely unlikely! However, holding your urine past the point of that "got-to-go" feeling may not be the best idea. Every person can ignore her or his body's signals to use the restroom for different amounts of time, but all of us have the same basic urinating instincts that will eventually prevail."[127]

### . . . to pee in the pool?

Everybody does it. But nobody should. According to the Water Quality and Health Council,[128] two out of every ten people swimming in American pools relieve themselves there, possibly in the mistaken belief that all that water will dilute their very small contribution. But when the uric acid in your urine meets the disinfectant chorine in the swimming pool, the result is cyanogen chloride and trichloramine. Yes, the concentration produced by one person peeing in the pool is unlikely to be hazardous. But worry-warts know that the first chemical is one that so effectively irritates the heart, lungs, and eyes that it has been used (in much larger amounts) in chemical warfare; the second is a skin irritant. Finally, a fair warning: Even if you don't admit to what you've done, your secret may not remain secret. Urine is a natural bleach that might just leave its telltale mark on your bathing suit.[129]

### . . . to pee on a jellyfish sting?

The skin and tentacles on a jellyfish (*Cnidaria Scyphozoa Aurelia*) are studded with cnidocytes, cells that contain nematocysts, specialized structures that emit venom to stun and capture prey. When a jellyfish hits you or you hit a jellyfish—*bang*! Instant pain, says Joseph Burnett of the University of Maryland Medical Center Consortium of Jellyfish Stings. Your best remedy is first to remove any tentacle clinging to your skin, gently so as not to trigger the nematocysts. Then, says Burnett, wash the injured area with salt water to deactivate any nematocysts still hanging on. No fresh water, please. Why? Osmosis. As you learned in Chemistry 101, this phenomenon is the "movement of a solvent (as water) through a semipermeable membrane (as of a living cell) into a solution of higher solute concentration that tends to equalize the concentrations of solute on the two sides of the membrane movement of a solvent (as water) through a semipermeable membrane (as of a living cell) into a solution of higher solute concentration that tends to equalize the concentrations of solute on the two sides of the membrane."[130] Fresh water is almost certainly less dense than the liquid inside the nematocyst. As the less dense fresh water flows into the cell, the denser liquid inside that cell will flow out on to your skin. More ouch. As for urine, Christopher Holstege, a toxicologist and professor of emergency medicine at the University of Virginia, says that if yours is very diluted, it will act just like plain fresh water. The better way is first to wash the site with the salty denser sea water. Once back on dry land, Holstege notes that most stings from jellyfish living in North American waters can be treated with acetic acid (vinegar) or a paste of baking soda and seawater.[131] Over-the-counter oral antiseptics can ease the pain, but ultimately your best friend is time which, healing all (or most) wounds, will do the trick.

### . . . to eat asparagus?

Asparagus may turn your urine smelly because digesting the veggies breaks its asparagusic acid into a bunch of stinky sulfur compounds such as methyl mercaptan. Exactly how offensive you find the odor may depend on whether you're a girl or a boy. When researchers at the Harvard T. H. Chan School of Public Health fed asparagus to 6,909 male and female volunteers and asked if their urine smelled different afterwards, 58 percent of the men said no. Among women, the no's were 3.5 percent higher. Their

## AROMA NOTE

Asparagus isn't the only food that makes urine smelly. Garlic does, too, and so do the various cruciferous vegetables such as cabbage, which also contain sulfur compounds. The odor is temporary, of course, but you can reduce its pungency by drinking lots of liquids with your asparagus.[133] Caution: That means drinking water, not coffee or alcohol. The latter two are diuretics, chemicals that make you pee more often, thus concentrating urine which makes it darker and stinkier.

conclusion? The inability to smell asparagus-scented urine is a specific kind of anosmia (lack of the sense of smell) due to "three independent markers" on chromosome 1, more common among men than among women.[132]

### . . . to smoke or chew tobacco?
No.

### . . . to bathe or shower?
Every year, more than 2.2 million Americans older than fifteen end up with an injury serious enough to send them to the nearest hospital Emergency Room. In 2008, the Centers for Disease Control and Prevention announced that 234,094 of these injuries happened in the bathroom, most frequently while bathing or showering. Most were due to a fall. No surprise there. Most were more common among people older than sixty-five. No surprise there, either. But here is a surprise: The problem was most likely to happen while a person was in or around the tub or climbing out rather than when climbing in because the primary hazard is a slippery floor. To reduce the risk, lay down non-skid mat strips in the shower/tub and a non-skid mat outside the tub so that you step out onto a dry surface. And install a grab bar in the wall for extra

insurance. In 2004, "The State of Home Safety in America" report from the Home Safety Council said that more than six of every ten United States homes were already using bathtub mats or non-skid strips, but fewer than two in ten had grab bars. Upping those numbers is likely to lower the number of injuries.[134]

## . . . to shower in the morning (or at night)?

Harvard psychologist Shelley Carson says that showering in the morning may create the meditative moment that allows you to solve a problem that was bothering you the night before. Morning showers are also a bonus for people who tend to cut themselves while shaving, she adds, because the human body experiences an a.m. surge of platelets, the particles that make blood clot faster, and thus require fewer bits of tissue on the face or legs. On the other hand, neurologist Christopher Winter, Medical Director of the Martha Jefferson Hospital Sleep Medicine Center in Charlottesville, Virginia, describes evening showers as excellent for those who need to wind down at the end of the day because "rapid cooling after you get out of the shower or out of the bath tends to be a natural sleep inducer." As an added extra bonus, the evening shower clincher may be that scrubbing down at night washes away the day's detritus, so you sleep cleaner, and so do your sheets.[135]

## . . . to shower during a thunderstorm?

It depends on the composition of the water pipes in your plumbing system. If they are made of metal, yes, lightning can theoretically hit the pipes and travel through them to sinks, faucets, showers, and tubs. But succumbing to your plumbing is rare and should be even more so in the future because modern construction often features non-conducting plastic PVC (polyvinyl chloride) pipes for indoor plumbing.[136]

## . . . to use the facility?

The tub, shower, and slippery floor aren't the only potential hazards in your bathroom. There is also the lowly—and sometimes very low—toilet that accounts for about 14 percent of the injuries that happen here triggered by a person's rising from the seat. The problem is simple physiology. Standing up after sitting for a while may cause postural hypotension, a sudden drop in blood pressure that makes a person feel light-headed or dizzy. Additionally, peeing, having

a bowel movement, or simply straining while doing so may trigger vasovagal syncope, a temporary and non-fatal feeling of faintness. This may occur at any age, but generally it is more common among older people. In 2008, the Centers for Disease Control and Prevention reported 266.6 incidents for every one hundred thousand people older than eighty-five vs. 4.1 per one hundred thousand people ages fifteen to twenty-four. So take your time getting up and consider putting a grab-bar next to the toilet for extra support when rising.[137]

## . . . to brush your teeth?

Remember "The Pothole," the *Seinfeld* episode that aired on February 20, 1997?

If not, it runs like this: Jerry accidentally knocks his girlfriend's toothbrush into the toilet. She uses it before he can warn her, after which he can't bring himself to kiss her. He plans secretly to "sterilize" her mouth, but before he can, she finds out what happened, knocks something of his into the toilet, and refuses to tell him what it is. "Seinfeldian" panic ensues, until eventually she names

# A Bristling Trade

William Addis (1734–1808) was an English rag trader jailed in 1770 for causing a riot. Exactly what set him off has been lost to history. But while in prison, unhappy cleaning his teeth with a rag, he is said to have saved a small bone from his evening meal, poked holes in the surface, stuck some pig's hair into the holes and glued them in place. Once free, Addis began manufacturing his invention; it became very popular and made him very rich. By 1840, Addis-type toothbrushes were being mass-produced around the world. In 1938, DuPont de Nemours took tooth brushes a big step forward with Dr. West's Miracle-Tuft Toothbrush®, the first one with softer, less-irritating nylon bristles. The first electric toothbrush, the Broxodent®, was invented in Switzerland in 1954 by Dr. Philippe Guy Woog; Sonex introduced the first ultrasonic brush in 1992. As for Addis, the company he started is now Wisdom Toothbrushes, still making its owners wealthy by turning out seventy million toothbrushes per year in the UK.[139]

the object: The toilet brush. What nobody told Jerry is that you don't have to knock your toothbrush into the toilet to contaminate it with unpleasant microorganisms. Begin with the fact that the brush comes to you in a sealed but not sterile package. Add to that the Staphylococci, coliform, pseudomonad, yeasts, and various intestinal bacteria bugs that live naturally in your mouth, hopping onto the brush every time you use it. Finally, and here's the gross part, it's a good bet your toothbrush is sitting in a holder on your sink which probably sits right next to the toilet which spews a fine particle mist into the air whenever you flush. To keep your brush clean and safe, the American Dental Association recommends swishing it with some anti-bacterial mouthwash before and after brushing, then rinsing the toothbrush with clean water and storing it—upright, uncovered, separated from other brushes on the sink—in open air to dry the bristles and make the brush less hospitable to the microbes that will inevitably drop in, one way or another. And, no, you should never share your brush. That's not selfish; it's dental common sense. You may be comfortable with what's already growing in your own mouth, but introducing foreign invaders can trigger an oral war.[138]

### . . . to brush with toothpaste?

Ever since man moved from a tooth-cleaning twig to a toothbrush, toothpaste and powder have made the brush taste good and increased its cleaning power. Generally speaking, these dentifrices are just fine. The exception would be if you are sensitive to an ingredient in the paste or powder such as fluoride or a flavoring which might trigger hives, rashes, "canker sores" (small ulcers), cracked lips, or even an upset stomach. In that case, your dentists might advise brushing with plain water or—if it won't abrade your dental apparatus—a baking soda/water paste.[140]

### . . . to brush with antibiotic toothpaste?

Triclosan is an antibiotic first introduced by surgeons who used it to "sterilize" their hands before heading into the operating room. In the 1990s, manufacturers began adding triclosan to everything from soap to toothpaste, after which animal studies suggested that triclosan may disrupt the normal development of the [fetal] reproductive system (human studies have not shown similar results). At the same time, it was clear that dentifrices with both triclosan and fluorides reduced the incidence of cavities, dental plaque, and bleeding or inflamed gums more effectively than fluorides alone which may be why when the Food and Drug Administration banned the use of Triclosan in face and body soaps in 2016, they left it in toothpaste. Should you be worried? Probably not. Dr. Richard Niederman, a dentist and the chairman of the epidemiology department at the New York University College of Dentistry, told *The New York Times*, but, he adds, if you're concerned, toothpaste with just "stannous fluoride is also very effective for reducing plaque and gingivitis."[141]

### . . . to floss your teeth?

Safe? Yes. Effective? Maybe. In August 2016, the American Periodontal Association stunned all Americans with teeth and gums when they announced that nobody had ever actually determined whether flossing really lowers the risk of cavities and gum disease because "researchers had not been able to include enough participants or 'examine gum health over a significant amount of time.'"[142] Nonetheless, the Association's website still says flossing "is an essential part of taking care of your teeth and gums."

The Mayo Clinic calls it more effective than a WaterPik®,[143] and Edmond R. Hewlett, professor of restorative dentistry at the University of California, Los Angeles, and ADA spokesman, says, "we're confident that disturbing the bacteria in plaque with brushing and flossing is, indeed, beneficial." Wayne Aldredge, APA president when the confusing study was released, still urges his patients to floss. Serious periodontal disease, he told Slate.com, is: "a very insidious, slow, bone-melting disease" that might creep up slowly without your knowing it's happening. Conclusion: Couldn't hurt to floss.[144]

## A Toothpick Record

There is a sport for every taste, every single one with a matching Guinness award for best or biggest or fastest or first. In September 2012, an Irishman named Ed Cahill earned his place in the record book by winning a contest to see how many toothpicks could be stuck fastest in a man's beard. Cahill's numbers: 3,107 toothpicks in less than three hours. .[147]

### . . . to use a toothpick?

Humans were using toothpicks even before they were fully humans. Both Neanderthal and Homo sapiens skulls show signs of teeth that were picked with some kind of tool. As society became more sophisticated, so did the picks. Bronze picks have been uncovered in prehistoric graves in Northern Europe. Some picks from the Middle Ages and after are works of art, sometimes set with precious stones, a stylized upper class way to rid oneself of bits of food caught between upper class teeth.[145] You could say that today we've gone backwards: The modern toothpick is a simple piece of wood, and the Mayo Clinic's modern dental advice is that "toothpicks are for *hors d'oeuvres*, not your teeth." To avoid injuring your gum and perhaps allowing bacteria to enter, Mayo advises plain floss, pre-threaded floss, brushes small enough to brush between your teeth, or a water-powered device.[146] Plus your trusty toothbrush, of course.

### . . . to use hand sanitizer?

As the World Health Organization frequently reminds us, "Clean hands save lives." American manufacturers have taken this to heart; you can't reach for anything in a drugstore these days without hitting a hand sanitizer. Now, the Food and Drug Administration has announced that they are beginning to look for scientific evidence proving that hand sanitizers and constant sanitizing are both safe and effective. In the meantime, the Food and Drug Administration acknowledges that the sanitizers are useful when you have no access to soap and running water, but says the latter is still the best way to wash away dirt and grease and also best at getting rid of germs by physically washing them away. In addition, while sanitizers do cut back the microbe population, they may not hit all types or bugs and overuse of a product with an antibiotic compound (in this case benzalkonium chloride) may create antibiotic resistant bugs.[148]

## How Not to Sanitize Your Mouth

Once upon a time, mothers might wash the mouths of trash-talking kids with soap and water. Today, Mom's big worry isn't the language; it's the fact that the kids may be washing their own mouths with alcohol-based hand sanitizers. In 2012, Anthony F. Suffredini of the National Institutes of Health reported that from 2005 through 2009 the number of people young and old who were drinking hand sanitizer climbed, in some cases dramatically, i.e., the number tripled both among children younger than nineteen and adults older than twenty.[149] In other words, for some kids, sneaking some sanitizer is more popular than sneaking into Mom and Dad's liquor cabinet.

## . . . to use the public restroom?

Surprise. It's not. The problem isn't the toilet. It's the faucet you turn on to wash your hands after using the facility. As with so many other public surfaces, the faucet has hosted dozens, maybe hundreds or thousands or millions of hands before yours. It's a conundrum: Which is more problematic, the faucet or the hand sanitizer? Decisions, decisions . . .

## Ten Times You Really Need to Wash Your Hands
- Before, during, and after preparing food
- Before eating food
- Before and after caring for someone who is sick
- Before and after treating a cut or wound
- After using the toilet
- After changing diapers or cleaning up a child who has used the toilet
- After blowing your nose, coughing, or sneezing
- After touching an animal, animal feed, or animal waste
- After handling pet food or pet treats
- After touching garbage[150]

## . . . to buy new glasses?

New spectacles generally improve your vision, which is why your optometrist or ophthalmologist prescribed them in the first place, but for senior citizens, the new prescriptions may increase the risk of tripping and falling. In 2014, vision experts at the University of Bradford (UK) reported that neither new glasses nor cataract surgery appear to reduce the incidence of falls among seniors. In fact, the numbers suggest that adjusting to new bi-focals or "progressive" multi-focal lenses may double the risk, perhaps because one tends to look down while climbing stairs or stepping across a curb. Doing that while wearing bi-focals means looking through the "close-up" lens normally used for reading, and that can blur the view of a step or curb. Ditto for progressives. To reduce the damage, the Bradford experts suggest getting two new pair of glasses, bifocal and progressive for home and indoor use; single lenses for outdoors.[151]

### . . . to "crack" your knuckles?

The sounds a knuckle-cracker makes may drive those around him crazy, but for the cracker it seems to be all good. In April 2015, researchers at the University of Alberta (Canada) reported that MRI images show the popping produced by cracking the joint is due to the collapse of air bubbles in the fluid around the joint. A while later, radiologists at the University of California Davis upped the game by using ultrasound machines—which are approximately one hundred times faster than MRIs—to track the cracking. "What we saw was a bright flash on ultrasound, like a firework exploding in the joint," said UCLA/Davis' Robert Boutin. Because the flashes occurred right along with the "popping" sound, his team believes that both are linked to changes in that fluid around the joint. How does this all affect a cracker's fingers? To everyone's surprise, when they compared crackers with non-crackers, they discovered, as Boutin says, that the former had "increased range of motion" due to the lubricating gas and fluid released by the "cracked" joints.

### . . . to wear a copper bracelet?

If you are sensitive to copper, the bracelet may make your wrist itch. Even if you're not sensitive to copper, the metal may turn your skin green-ish because when it's exposed to air it oxidizes, undergoing chemical reactions that create a patina, a layer of pale green cells that rub off on your skin. Otherwise, no problem, but no remedy for arthritis either. Old (or New) Wives' Tales to the contrary, a controlled, double-blind British study in 2013 is just the latest in a long line to find that copper bracelets are no more effective against arthritis than a placebo.[152]

### . . . to go to sleep?

Usually, yes. One notable exception appears to be some people with sleep apnea, a condition in which a loss of cells in the pre-Bötzinger complex—an area of the brain that controls respiration—triggers a pause in breathing. In most cases, the sleeper awakens with a start, but not in all cases. As a result, researchers at the University of California in Los Angeles (UCLA) suspect that some elderly patients or people in the late stages of neurodegenerative disorders, who were thought to have suffered a heart attack while sleeping, may actually have succumbed to sleep apnea. The next step for the UCLA team is to analyze the brains of people who die from neurodegenerative diseases to determine whether these patients show damage in that brain command post for generating breathing in mammals.[153] Halfway around the world, researchers from Chosun University Hospital, Seoul National University College of Medicine and the Seoul National University Bundang Hospital are pursuing similar studies. Previous efforts have concentrated on Western populations, but the Korean research seems to show similar effects among Asians.[154]

### . . . to skip some sleep #1?

The average adult dog sleeps twelve to fourteen hours a day, although that may vary with his age and breed. An average adult cat may snooze as long as sixteen hours of every twenty-four hours, mostly during the day like her wild cousins who sleep all day and hunt all night which, in domestic terms, means waking you up at

# All Through the Night

The fear of slipping away while sleeping appears to be universal among humans from childhood on, as shown by the classic prayer some children recite to keep them safe until morning:

"Now I lay me down to sleep,
I pray the Lord my soul to keep,
If I should die before I wake,
I pray the Lord my soul to take."

These four simple lines, from the 1750 edition of *The New England Primer*, the first made-in-America reading textbook, are so famous that they have made their way, more or less, into the music of (in alphabetical order) such varied artists as Aerosmith, Aloe Blacc, Christina Aguilera, Frank Wilson, Frankie Knuckles & Jamie Principle, G-Eazy, HIM, Kanye West, Kid Cudi, Lucky Dube, Megadeth, Metallica, Notorious B.I.G., OPM, Pirates of the Mississippi, Sky Ferreira, Snoop Dogg, TobyMac, and Sweethearts of the Rodeo.[155]

None of these musicians, however, have used Shel Silverstein's rather darker "Prayer of A Selfish Child" from *Light in the Attic* (1981):

"Now I lay me down to sleep,
I pray the Lord my soul to keep,
And if I die before I wake,
I pray the Lord my toys to break.
So none of the other kids can use 'em . . .
Amen."[156]

3 a.m. demanding food. Adult humans, on the other hand, generally run on a day-awake/night-asleep schedule which the National Sleep Foundation says includes between seven and ten hours sleep. Cutting back can be problematic. People who torture other people to extract information or sometimes just for the heck of it, know that keeping a person awake for long periods of time renders him or her more or less helpless. Without a renewal time-out, the brain cannot concentrate. Both short- and long-term memory suffer, as does balance, the immune system, and the cardiovascular apparatus. A sleep-deprived person may be anxious, depressed, angry, or even temporarily suicidal. He may also gain weight because the sleep-deprived brain can't tell the body that it (the body) has had enough to eat. Finally, lacking sufficient sleep time, a person may drive her car into a wall or over a cliff. In 2016, based on data from 4,571 crashes between July 2005 and December 2007, the AAA Foundation for Traffic Safety concluded that drivers who missed as little as one of the recommended seven hours' sleep a night were a 1.3 times more likely to be involved in an accident. Missing two hours raised that to twice as likely. "Managing a healthy work-life balance can be difficult, and far too often, we sacrifice our sleep as a result," said Jake Nelson, director of Traffic Safety Advocacy and Research for AAA. "Failing to maintain a healthy sleep schedule could mean putting yourself or others on the road at risk."[157]

## . . . to skip some sleep #2?

In 2017, a North American Menopause Society (NAMS) survey of more than ninety thousand older women showed that those who got less than seven to eight hours of sleep each night were more likely to say their sex life was unsatisfactory. But don't blame that on their age. As Krystal Woodbridge, a trustee of the College of Sexual and Relationship Therapists (COSRT) says, "Sleep is key to good health full stop. Sleep is essential for regulating hormones, which affect many aspects of our health and therefore how we feel physically, how we feel about ourselves and our partners, and sex."[158] At any age.

| How Many Hours Should You Sleep? | | | |
|---|---|---|---|
| Age | Recommended | May be appropriate[159] | Not recommended[160] |
| Newborns 0-3 months | 14-17 | 11-13/18 -19 | <11/ >19 |
| Infants 4-11 months | 12-15 | 10-11/16-18 | <10/>18 |
| Toddlers 1-2 years | 11-14 | 9-10/15-16 | <9/>16 |
| Preschool 3-5 years | 10-13 | 8-9/9-14 | <8/>14 |
| School age 6-13 years | 9-11 | 7-8 /12 | <7/>12 |
| Teen 14-17 years | 8-10 | 7-11 | <7/>11 |
| Young Adults 18-25 years | 7-9 | 6-10/10-11 | <6/>11 |
| Adults 26-64 years | 7-9 | 6/10 | <6/>10 |
| Older Adults 65+ years | 7-8 | 5-6/9 | <5/>9 |

# 4
# Sports & Other Athletic Endeavors

"Sports do not build character.
They reveal it."

—Heywood Hale Broun (1888-1939)

## Is it safe to stretch your muscles?

The American College of Sports Medicine says regular stretching of your eight major muscle groups, particularly in your lower back and upper thighs, helps to maintain the ability to move smoothly as you grow older. The ACSM recommendation is to do static stretches (reaching up or out or back without moving) three times a week, reaching as far as comfortable and holding

## The Major 8
*Back and shoulders*: deltoid & trapezius
*Arm*: biceps and triceps
*Chest*: pectoralis major
*Abdominals*: rectus abdominis and internal oblique
*Back*: erector spinae, latissimus dorsi & rhomboideus
*Buttocks*: gluteus maximus
*Thighs*: quadriceps and hamstrings
*Calves*: gastrocnemius and soleus

the position for ten to thirty seconds for each stretch. A second exercise, called the dynamic stretch, means moving while stretching. For example, you raise your arms above your head for a few seconds, then lace your fingers and reach out in front and then stretch backwards, only as far as it is comfortable for you and only for a few seconds at a time.[161]

### . . . to stretch before you exercise?

It's a mixed bag. There's no evidence to show that static stretches before exercising improves performance or prevents injury. In fact, there are actual studies showing just the opposite, particularly for sprinters, perhaps because they "tire" the muscles in advance of the run. On the other hand, dynamic stretches such as swinging your legs or walking briskly are useful warm-ups for the main event. After exercise, when circulation to your muscles and joints has increased, stretching is a good way to round out the workout.[162] Here's a third possibility: Stretching is an adaptable exercise in itself. If you don't run, jump, skip, hop, or lift weights on a regular schedule, you can do your stretching anytime—when you wake up, as a lunch-time or mid-afternoon break from your desk job, or right before you go to bed.

### . . . to stand on one leg?

That depends on where and why you're doing it. As every toddler demonstrates, standing up on two legs is hard to do, requiring constant and continuing small adjustments to your balance. Walking or running is exponentially more complicated. You have to push off with your foot (actually the big toe), bounce back and forth on your ankles, and lift and extend and lower your knee, all in an unconsciously coordinated and perfectly smooth sequence that some have described as "controlled falling." Pause in mid-step and you are likely to trip and fall. Maintaining your equilibrium while performing these gymnastics involves your eyes and your ears as well as your muscles and bones. You need your eyes to let you see where you're going while nerve cells in semicircular canals within your inner ear behave like a gyroscope, helping you to keep your balance when you move your head from side to side or up and down. Your muscles and bones must be strong enough to support your weight and must react fast enough to accommodate sudden glitches such as a bump on the sidewalk that could trip you up and send you face first to the ground. As you grow older, these balance enablers tend to weaken, which is where standing on one leg comes in. Any exercise that keeps you moving is good for helping to maintain balance, but standing on one leg is particularly so. The first time you try, you may not even make ten seconds, but practice makes perfect progress. It is easier to stay balanced if you keep your eyes on a fixed horizon, but stay with it, eventually you may even be able to stand there, perched on one leg like a stork, while looking around the room or even with your eyes closed.[163]

## . . . to play football?

Heads up: During the 2012 National Football League season, the PBS program *Frontline* ran a project called "Concussion Watch," eventually identifying 161 players temporarily out of action due to a head injury or a concussion.[164] Three years later, the number had risen to 199.[165] Professionals aren't the only ones at risk. In 2014, the *American Journal of Sports Medicine* reported that the rate of concussions among high school athletes, boys and girls, had more

# Whose Head Hurts

*NFL concussions by team position 2015*[167]

### OFFENSE

Wide receiver: . . . . . . . . . . . . . . . . . . . . . . . . . . . . . .24
Tight end: . . . . . . . . . . . . . . . . . . . . . . . . . . . . . .17
Tackle: . . . . . . . . . . . . . . . . . . . . . . . . . . . . . .15
Quarterback: . . . . . . . . . . . . . . . . . . . . . . . . . . . . . .12
Running back: . . . . . . . . . . . . . . . . . . . . . . . . . . . . . .11
Guard: . . . . . . . . . . . . . . . . . . . . . . . . . . . . . .10
Center: . . . . . . . . . . . . . . . . . . . . . . . . . . . . . .9

### DEFENSE

Cornerback: . . . . . . . . . . . . . . . . . . . . . . . . . . . . . .41
Linebacker: . . . . . . . . . . . . . . . . . . . . . . . . . . . . . .24
Safety: . . . . . . . . . . . . . . . . . . . . . . . . . . . . . .17
End: . . . . . . . . . . . . . . . . . . . . . . . . . . . . . .10
Tackle: . . . . . . . . . . . . . . . . . . . . . . . . . . . . . .7

# Whose Head Hurts, Junior Edition[168]

*Number of concussion per one hundred thousand
"athletic exposures" (one athlete taking part in one organized
high school athletic practice or competition)*

Football: . . . . . . . . . . . . . . . . . . . . . . . . . . . . . 64–76.8
Boys' ice hockey: . . . . . . . . . . . . . . . . . . . . . . . . .54
Boys' lacrosse: . . . . . . . . . . . . . . . . . . . . . . . . 40–46.6
Girls' soccer: . . . . . . . . . . . . . . . . . . . . . . . . .33
Girls' lacrosse: . . . . . . . . . . . . . . . . . . . . . . . . .31–35
Boys' wrestling: . . . . . . . . . . . . . . . . . . . . . . . . 22–23.9
Girls' field hockey: . . . . . . . . . . . . . . . . . . . . . . . . 22–24.9
Boys' soccer: . . . . . . . . . . . . . . . . . . . . . . . . 19–19.2
Girls' basketball: . . . . . . . . . . . . . . . . . . . . . . . . 18.6–21
Girls' softball: . . . . . . . . . . . . . . . . . . . . . . . . 16–16.3
Boys' basketball: . . . . . . . . . . . . . . . . . . . . . . . . 16–21.2
Cheerleading: . . . . . . . . . . . . . . . . . . . . . . . . 11.5–14
Girls' gymnastics: . . . . . . . . . . . . . . . . . . . . . . . . .7
Girls' volleyball: . . . . . . . . . . . . . . . . . . . . . . . . .6– 8.6
Boys' baseball: Between . . . . . . . . . . . . . . . . . . . . 4.6–5

than doubled in the eight years from 2005 to 2012. "We don't know the exact reasons," said Joseph Rosenthal of Ohio State University. Is it that that high school sports have become more dangerous? Rosenthal says, probably not. His more likely explanation: High school coaches, athletes, and their parents have become more aware of the possibility of head injuries, and that, he concludes, is "good news."[166]

### . . . to kick a ball?

Surreptitiously tapping that golf ball into the hole doesn't count. Kicking a pigskin or soccer ball does, although given all the tackling and slamming, you'd think a simple kick would be relatively harmless. It isn't. When you kick, your hip and knee joints flex as your thigh and back muscles stretch and strain and sometime even tear in the effort to move that ball. Here's the physical sequence:

1. The gluteus muscles in your buttock pull your leg back to flex your hip joint.

2. Simultaneously, the hamstring muscle on the back of your thigh flexes your knee joint.

3. The gastrocnemius muscle on the back of your leg below the knee flexes your ankle joint.

4. The iliopsoas (inner hip) muscle flexes the hip joint as it begins to move forward.

5. The quadriceps muscles (rectus femoris, vastus medialis, vastus lateralis, vastus intermedialis) on the front of your thigh extends your knee.

6. The gastroncnemius once again flexes your ankle and *boom*! You kick the ball.

Obviously, all this action creates many opportunities to damage a muscle or joint. The good news is that in most cases while that may be painful or even temporarily disabling, it is rarely life threatening.[169]

## . . . to head a ball?

Like American football players, soccer players are forbidden from hitting each other with their heads. But heading—hitting the soccer ball with your head—is de rigueur, so while as many as four of every five soccer injuries are to the legs and feet, one study from Central Hospital in Rogaland (Norway) puts head injuries at between 4 and 22 percent. As in football, leg and foot injuries may put a player out of commission for a while, but head injuries may have devastating consequences. Even "minor" head trauma may lead to organic brain damage and a long list of other problems, including "headache, dizziness, irritability, impaired memory and neck pain," along with abnormal EEG, central cerebral atrophy, mild to severe (mostly mild to moderate) neuropsychological impairment, and a significantly higher incidence and degree of degenerative changes in the cervical spine.[170] The most common cause (no surprise here) is getting hit in the head with the ball,

**Annual number of injuries per sport[172]**

Basketball: 512,213
Bicycling: 485,669
Football: 418,260
Soccer: 174,686
Baseball: 155,898
Skateboards: 112,544
Trampolines: 108,029
Softball: 106,884
Swimming/Diving: 82,354
Horseback riding: 73,576
Weightlifting: 65,716
Volleyball: 52,091
Golf: 47,360
Roller skating: 35,003
Wrestling: 33,734

particularly one kicked by somebody close by and traveling at 62 miles/100 kilometers per hour, so fast that there's no time to duck. Adult players are on their own, but to protect young athletes, experts recommend "no heading" rules on the totally sensible theory that if a player is not allowed to head the ball, the ball is less likely to hit a player's head.[171]

### . . . to lead a cheer?

Cheerleading ranks astronomically high on the injury meter. Data released in 2008 from a twenty-five-year study by the National Center for Catastrophic Sports Injury Research at the University of North Carolina shows that cheerleading accounts for nearly-seven of every ten "catastrophic" injuries among high school and college female athletes. The numbers have increased as the sport has continued to become more popular. According to the United States Consumer Product Safety Commission (CPSC), about twenty-five thousand cheerleaders are sent to emergency rooms each year, a number that has risen more than 600 percent over the past twenty years. The only answer, one researcher noted, is to put in place safety regulations as stringent as those for other contact sports.

### . . . to shoot some hoops?

If you think football is our most hazardous sport, think again. Except for concussions, in which football clearly leads the leagues, the sport that sends most Americans to the emergency room is basketball. More than five hundred thousand players made the trip in 2005. That's about 25 percent more than the four hundred thousand laid low by football.

### . . . to hunt and shoot?

For you and your hunting buddies, it's safe so long as you follow all the rules. Primary among them is the need to positively

identify the target before pulling the trigger or letting an arrow fly. Unfortunately, this simple stratagem appears to escape many American hunters who every year fatally wound dozens of other hunters, by-standers, and even themselves.[173]

## . . . to pack a pistol in your home?

The National Rifle Association is right. Guns don't kill people. People kill people, by accident more often than you might think. In America, your lifetime odds of dying from an accidental gunshot are 1 in 7,994.[174] In 2000, the American Academy of Pediatrics, whose membership must certainly include hunters and target shooters, asked all pediatricians to ask parents to keep their home a gun-free zone. Eleven years later, combing through reports of all gun injuries between 2003 and 2007, David Hemenway, director of the Harvard Injury Control Research explained why. His study documented about 680 accidental fatal shootings every year, half the victims—friends, relatives, or the gun owner him or herself—were younger than twenty-five. As Hemenway noted, the main reason people give for having a handgun in the home is protection, typically against "stranger violence." In reality, home is relatively safe from strangers. Fewer than one-third of burglaries occur when someone's home is broken into, and when the event turns violent, it's likely that "burglar" is someone the homeowner knows and dislikes, such as an ex-spouse.[175]

## Guns vs. Doctors

In 2011, the Florida state legislature passed the Firearm Owners' Privacy Act, barring doctors from discussing gun safety with their patients. Citing the First Amendment's guarantee of free speech, as well as the relationship between doctor and patient, the medical men and women went to court. Six years later, the law was declared unconstitutional by the United States Circuit Court of Appeals for the 11th Circuit, a decision applauded by the plaintiffs who included the American College of Physicians, the Florida Chapter ACP, the Florida Pediatric Society/ Florida Chapter of the American Academy of Pediatrics, the American Academy of Family Physicians, and a whole long list of individual Florida doctors.[176]

## . . . to ski or snowboard?

Sliding down a mountain isn't the world's most dangerous sport. True, it accounts for hundreds, probably thousands of broken, sprained, or twisted limbs each year, but cycling is Number One on the "Hazardous Scale." In 2001, amateur cyclists racked up 900 deaths, 23,000 hospital admissions, 580,000 emergency department visits and more than 1.2 million physician visits per year in the United States.[177] That doesn't mean the winter stuff is for sissies. Even if you do everything right, each year more than 100,000 avalanches roll down around the world's slopes, accounting for about 150 deaths. During the 2015-2016 season in the United States alone, sliding snow killed thirty skiers, snowboarders, snowmobilers, and snowshoe hikers in the Western United States. To protect yourself, stay on the main path, travel single file, and always have a partner with you to dig you out if the snow slides.[178]

## . . . to ride a bicycle?

See previous entry.

## . . . to swim alone?

What works for skiing, works for swimming: Don't do it alone. The American Red Cross says you should always have a buddy, even in a pool where the mass of swimmers may conceal one who's in trouble or on a lifeguarded beach because even lifeguards have moments when they look away.

# 5

# Fashion & Beauty

"Taking joy in living is a woman's best cosmetic."

—Rosalind Russell (1907-1976)

### Is it safe to Botox® your wrinkles?

When you inject a paralytic poison into your face, you may not be able to smile or frown for a while, but other than that, really, what could go wrong?

Plenty. Botulinum toxin (BTX) is the neurotoxin produced by Clostridium botulinum, an anaerobic bacterium that thrives in low-acid environments with little or no available oxygen, like the inside of a poorly sterilized can of green beans. There are seven different types of BTX, labeled A to G. The A, which can make you really sick or even kill you if you get them in your food, is used medically in products such as Botox Cosmetic® and Botox®, in very low dosages designed to relax muscle spasms in various parts of your body such as your forehead or your bladder. Using cosmetic Botox® to relax frown lines between your eyes or wipe away "crow's feet" is generally regarded as side-effect free, but there are exceptions. Right off the bat, or needle, you might be allergic to the chemical which may trigger itching, rash, red itchy welts, wheezing, asthma symptoms, or dizziness. Hours or days or even weeks after the Botoxing, you may experience symptoms of botulism such as double or blurred vision, drooping eyelids, or trouble breathing or swallowing that may become so severe that you need a feeding tube to receive food and water. Happily, Allergen, the company that markets BOTOX®, notes that to date "there has not been a confirmed serious case of spread of toxin effect away from the injection site when BOTOX® has been used at the recommended dose to treat chronic migraine, severe underarm sweating, blepharospasm (involuntary closing of the eyelids), or strabismus, or when BOTOX® Cosmetic has been used at the recommended dose to treat frown lines and/or crow's feet lines."[179] Which is nice, but what Italian actress Anna Magnani (1908-1973) once said is safer, more self-assured, and much less expensive: "Don't retouch my wrinkles. It took me so long to earn them."

## . . . to polish your nails?

With few exceptions, all nail polish sold in the United States contains a "toxic trio" of three potentially hazardous chemicals: formaldehyde (a hardener), toluene (a solvent), and dibutyl phthalate/DBT (a plasticizer that makes the polish shiny). The first is a known carcinogen; the second and third are reported to cause developmental defects. The European Union has banned the use of DBP in cosmetics. The Food and Drug Administration has not, even though some experts worry that the ingredients might be absorbed through the nail onto and into your skin and body—a concern amplified in 2015 when a Duke University/ Environmental Working Group study found that within fourteen hours after polishing their nails, a group of fourteen female volunteers had increased levels of diphenyl phosphate/DTHP in their bodies. DTHP, created when your body metabolizes triphenyl phosphate, another plasticizer, is an endocrine disrupter, a chemical that interferes with the body's natural production of hormones.[180] Consumer alert: You can find a list of polishes without the toxic trio at The Environmental Working Group's searchable cosmetics database, www.ewg.org/skindeep.

## . . . to get a manicure?

Having someone else bedazzle your finger and toe nails can be a luxury, but it can be expensive, more so for the manicurist than for you. As a savvy consumer, it's your job is to make sure that the salon you visit is licensed as required in your state and that it is clean, meaning that the staff washes hands between customers and the instruments used to poke around your nails are sterilized or disposable. You are in and out in a relatively short time, but salon workers are stuck there, doing nail after nail, hand after hand, for several hours a day several days a week, exposed to the polish and its vapor for long periods of time. The result may be headaches, dizziness, irritated skin, eyes, nose and throat, coughing, nausea, vomiting, and potential damage to a developing fetus, a list of symptoms that has prompted several states to pass new regulations to protect these workers.[181]

## . . . to gel your nails?

Varnish is a finish such as the shellac applied to wood and other surfaces to make them hard, shiny, and more or less damage-proof. Gel nail polish is a special varnish whose main attraction is that it may last as long as two weeks without chipping. The drawback is that gel polishes are "cured" (dried) with lamps that emit ultraviolet light, the radiation that may cause skin cancer if you stay out too long in the sun. While one study from Massachusetts General Hospital puts the risk of malignancies due to these lamps at "Not 'no risk,' but 'low risk,'" even if you use one once a week for 250 years,[182] some dermatologists suggest applying sunscreen to the top of your hands and fingers before a gel polishing.[183]

## . . . to wear fake nails?

Type "fingernails" and "sexy" into your computer search bar, and you'll see that long nails on female fingers are considered seductive. If you can't grow your own, acrylic paste-ons are an available substitute, but this alternative is far from perfect. The resins in the acrylic may cause redness and swelling at the fingertip, sometime severe enough to separate the underlying natural nail from its bed. Damage the plastic nail and you may create a gap between it and your own nail, in which bacteria may thrive. Even if all goes well, the Mayo Clinic suggests removing the acrylic nails every second or third month to allow your own nails to breathe.[184]

## . . . to nibble on your nails?

Onychophagia, from the Greek words *onyx* meaning "nail" or "claw" and *-phagia* meaning "eat," is a common stress-reliever, most likely among children and after age ten, more frequent among boys than girls.[187] Bitten nails are definitely not pretty. The edges of the nails are likely to be ragged and the skin around the nail is commonly red, raw, and susceptible to infection. Long-term nail-biting may also interfere with normal nail growth, sometimes leading to producing oddly shaped nails. Unless you wash your hands before biting, chewing your nails also means chewing anything you've touched. The good news is that nail biting rarely causes serious medical problems, and unless it's linked to another problem such as obsessive/compulsive disorder (OCD), most nail-biters outgrow the habit by around age thirty. One caveat: Children may be particularly susceptible to phthalates in nail polish, so some pediatricians warn against letting young nail-biters wear nail polish.

## Mirror, mirror, on the wall, Who's got the longest nails of all?

The wicked Queen in *Snow White* was actually asking the Magic Mirror to tell her who was the prettiest lady in the land, but you can bet she also had killer fingernails. In real life, the longest ever grown on both hands, male or female, belonged to American Lee Redmond who started growing her nails in 1979 and managed to get them to 28'4.5"/967.74 cm right up until early 2009 when she lost the prize-winners in an automobile accident.[185] The record-holder for the longest nails on one hand is Shridhar Chillal from India, who stopped cutting them in 1952. His extraordinary thumb nail: 6'5"/197.8 cm.[186]

### . . . to blow dry your hair?

Repeated blow-drying may dry your hair, and if the dryer runs too hot, defined as more than 140°F/60°C, you may actually singe both your curly locks and your scalp. To protect you from a dryer gone wild, the entire appliance is insulated so your hand doesn't heat, and virtually all dryers now have safety cutoff switches and/or thermal fuses to shut down the motor if the temperature accidentally rises above safe levels. As a result, while killing off a bather by tossing a turned-on or hair dryer into the tub has been

standard fare for murder movies and TV shows, the method may be soon be outdated. Many modern bathtubs are filled through plastic rather than electricity-conducting copper pipes. Additionally, modern dryers come equipped with a Ground Fault Circuit Interrupter (GFCI)—that big, three-prong polarized plug that monitors the current running from one opening in your wall outlet and then back into another. If the GFCI senses a problem, it trips the circuit and shuts down the electricity. Nonetheless, you definitely still should not touch a working radio or dryer that tumbles into the tub. The simpler, safer way to avoid an unpleasant electrical incident is to wash your hair, step out of the tub or shower, towel off, and then dry your hair while listening to news or music on your favorite station broadcasting over a totally dry radio.[188]

### . . . to try to save a drowned dryer?

No. If an unplugged dryer falls into water in your sink or tub, lift it out, and toss it. If you stand near a tub and drop a plugged one in, unplug the dryer without touching it or putting your hands into the water. Turn off the shower or drain the tub (again without putting your hands in the water). Lift the dryer out and throw it away or recycle it. Even if you leave it out to dry forever, you can't see inside the case where it's likely that water that has seeped inside and will eventually corrode the dryer's innards. Do not pry the case open and attempt to repair it. Instead, give the drowning victim a decent burial, and replace it with a new one.

## . . . to dye your hair?

The story for hair dye safety is similar to the one for nail polish: Generally safe for you, but not so much for salon workers. In 1979, the Food and Drug Administration tried to force hair-coloring makers whose products included 4-methoxy-m-phenylenediamine (4-MMPD), a suspected carcinogen, to put a warning label on the package saying "Contains an ingredient that can penetrate your skin and has been determined to cause cancer in laboratory animals." The agency had the studies to prove its

# Minerals, Nuts, Herbs & Coal

Once upon a time, people darkened their hair with solutions of tree bark or herbs or metallic compounds or ground walnut shells (active ingredient: pyrogallol) or they went blonde via a mixture of quicklime and wood ash or red with henna or a sulfur, "rock alum" (potassium) and honey paste. The first chemical hair coloring agent was hydrogen peroxide ($H_2O_2$) in 1818. It was marketed seventy-one years later at the Exhibition Universelle in Paris in 1889, *eau de fontaine de jouvence* (fountain of youth water), perhaps the first explicit statement that coloring your hair might make you look younger. In 1888, German chemist Ernst Erdmann patented p-Phenylenediamine, the first permanent "coal tar" (petroleum-based) dye. In 1910, French hairdresser, Gaston Boudou created the first line of standardized hair dyes that produced predictable colors. These new products also produced predictable adverse effects (allergic reactions) and the possibility of more serious long-term damage (cancer).[191] Clairol introduced the first no-mess, no-fuss dyes in 1950, and within twenty years, the percentage of American women dying their hair zoomed up from 8 percent to 50 percent.[192] Today, estimates are that seven of every ten American women use some form of hair coloring.[193]

point, but manufacturers stood their ground, the Food and Drug Administration backed down, and to everyone's surprise, manufactures soon stopped using it anyway although they continued to insist it had been safe. Science still says otherwise: A 2001 paper in the *International Journal of Cancer* concludes that women who frequently dye their hair are twice as likely to develop bladder cancer as those who don't.[189] The number of times you dye your hair and the color you use may affect your risk. A 2001 report from the University of California says that coloring your hair with permanent dye at least once a month for a year or longer doubles the odds of your developing bladder cancer. At fifteen years, the risk triples. For salon workers, the risk doubles in just one year. Using a dark shade eight times or more a year for more than twenty-five years doubles your risk of non-Hodgkins lymphoma. Blonde bleaches? No such effect. They don't add color.[190]

## . . . to wrap yourself in plastic?

Water has weight, so when you perspire and lose water, you also lose a pound or two or maybe more after a serious workout. The loss, of course, is temporary. Replace the water, and your weight will return to normal. Nonetheless, in the attempt to lose weight fast, some spas and consumers endorse wrapping your body with plastic sheets, sometimes plastic dipped in a magic herbal potion that "detoxifies" as it makes you sweat. Unfortunately, as serious athletes and medical professionals know, profuse sweating may lead to dehydration which may lead to weakness, dizziness, and confusion. Carried to extremes it

may even lead to coma and death, as once happened in Sedona, Arizona, in 2009 when three people died during a sweat lodge "purification" ritual and the man who ran the deadly show went to jail for two years.[194] Even though "spa" attendants aren't skilled medicine men and women, that's unlikely to happen with a fast spa wrap, but neither will the wrap burn off your fat. All you'll lose is water (temporarily) plus the cost of the procedure, about $160 per wrap, once a week, forever and ever. Diet and exercise anyone?[195]

### . . . to pierce your earlobes?

Millions of women for thousands of years in dozens of countries say, "Yes." The modern proviso, of course, is that whoever does the piercing must follow standard sanitary medical procedure. The shop should be clean. The piercer should be licensed and vaccinated against hepatitis B (your own tetanus vaccination should be up to date). The piercers should wash their hands between clients and wear disposable gloves. The tools should be sterilized or used only once, and tossed into a "waste" bag when done; no "piercing gun" allowed. To reduce the risk of infection and allergic reactions, the jewelry or studs should be made of surgical steel, solid gold, or platinum. After that, you need to keep the wound clean. When it heals: Diamonds anyone?[196]

### . . . to "pixie" your ears?

Pixies are imaginary creatures—small, often female, with magical powers and ears pointed at the top, similar to those of the Greek god Pan, whose pictures show ears rivaling Mr. Spock's. As for Spock himself, *Star Trek* made his ears so famous that enthusiastic Trekkies often took their own to "body modifiers," who sliced apart the cartilage at the top of the ear's outer rim (the helix) and then stitched it back together into a point. Reputable plastic surgeons wince at the practice which, like all other surgery is both risky and, unlike ear lobe piercings, irreversible. However, there is always the options of plastic overlays that, for less than $7 a pair are described as working well as "both Vulcan and Romulan ears" and are an "Officially licensed Star Trek costume accessory. . . perfect for the new or classic Star Trek fan."[197]

## . . . to pierce your tongue?

Unlike your earlobes, which are right out there in the open or your nostril which is pretty much so, your tongue is inside your mouth, so anything you do to it may affect the entire oral cavity. First, there's the possibility that your tongue may swell to block your throat. Next, there's the risk of infection by the trillions of bacteria that normally live in your mouth. After that, you may have to check of a list of unpleasant events linked to the jewelry itself. Start with periodontal disease due to jewels hitting your gums. Continue with damaged teeth, a problem experienced by as many as 40 percent of people with a tongue ornament. And last but by no means least, how about coping with a jewel whose placement complicates or confuses future diagnostic dental X-rays or one that comes loose so that you swallow or maybe choke on it. The same list of nasties may occur with other oral piercings such as your uvula (the knob of tissue hanging down at the entrance to you throat) and your lip.[198] Clearly this explains why the American Dental Association cautions against oral piercings, labeling them "invasive procedures with negative health sequelae that outweigh any potential benefit."[199]

## . . . to double pierce your tongue?

Think of this as double trouble. "Snake eyes," a.k.a. horizontal tongue piercing, looks like two separate inserts but is really one curved anchor that emerges at two separate openings in your tongue, one at either end of the bar. The anchor may push or smash together muscles that move your tongue. Its placement is also problematic because both the anchor and the ornaments sit in back of your teeth, perfectly positioned to bang against the teeth, possibly chipping and cracking the enamel.[200]

## . . . to split your tongue?

The scientific word for this is bifurcate from the Latin *bi-* meaning "two" and *furca* meaning "fork." It is done by using a scalpel to cut your tongue down or up the middle to separate it into two sections. The American Dental Association warns that doing this comes with a "significant" risk of bleeding, inflammation, infection, and possible damage to the nerves that control the tongue's movements thus possibly interfering with speech.[201] Whether bifurcation is legal and who can do it varies from country to country and even from state to state. In 2003, the state of Illinois said only licensed physicians could split a tongue. New York, Delaware, and Texas have since passed laws requiring the procedure to be done only by a licensed physician or dentist, and in 2009, the Australian state of Victoria banned all tongue-splitting for minors, no matter who did it.[202]

## . . . to pierce your navel?

Piercing an earlobe or a tongue means pushing the piercer through from one side of the surface to the other, which means it's possible to post in place with a jewel on top and a kind of stopper at the back. Not so with your navel where no through-and-through piercing is possible. So this decoration requires a dermal anchor, a small piece of sterile metal inserted into a hole punched in the skin and then held firmly in place by the tissue that naturally grows back around it. The problem is that "firmly" may be a debatable term. Dermal anchors are foreign objects that may be rejected by your body. They may "migrate" or become dislodged if they catch on your clothes, the latter most commonly before the puncture is completely healed. Even if they stay in place, they may cause prominent scarring.[203] Finally, you can't just saunter down to your local mall and pick one up or stick one in. Although dermal anchors are not regulated by the FDSA, they are "classified as class 1 devices, for use by medical professionals only. State medical boards determine who can use each classification of products, and what level of certification, education and/or competency testing each user must have. *Unless your local health department or medical board specifically allows the use of class 1 devices by body art practitioners, the use of punches by body art practitioners is prohibited.*"[204]

### . . . to pierce your private parts?

Leaving aside the questionable value of constant erotic irritation, all the cautions applied to other piercings apply here as well. That is, if you can leave aside the questionable value of constant erotic irritation.

### . . . to tattoo?

Once taboo, tattoos are now tres chic, from a delicate rose where the sun don't shine to fake permanent eyebrows, eyeliner, lip liner, and the blush on a female cheek. But as the number of tattooed faces and bodies rises, so does the concern about potential risks such as itchy or reddened skin due to exposure to sunlight, temporary swelling or burning at the site after an MRI, infections from unsterilized needles, scarring, and allergies to pigments in both temporary and permanent tattoos. Your state and local authorities write the rules on who can do the tattoo, but the Food and Drug Administration has the right to regulate the inks. To date, the agency has not actually approved any pigments for tattoo injections into your skin, but responding to recent reports of problems linked to permanent tattoos, Food and Drug Administration and its National Center for Toxicological Research (NCTR) are beginning to look into how chemicals in the inks may affect your body. Preliminary info from NCTR suggests that some pigment migrates from the tattoo site to the body's lymph nodes. How this may (or may not) affect your health is still a mystery. Until the agencies decide what is or isn't safe, Food and Drug Administration's advice is pure poetry: "Think before you ink."[205]

### . . . to remove your tatts at home?

This is definitely a Do-It-Yourself Don't. Permanent tattoos inject colored ink below the skin's surface, which is why they are permanent. If you second guess your decision and decide to remove the tattoo, you are in for a time-consuming, costly, doesn't-always-work experience that most commonly involves repeated laser treatments. Trying to do it yourself will likely be unsuccessful. The Food and Drug Administration has not approved the acid-based products meant for home use, which it says may seriously irritate your skin. Another reason to think before you ink comes from two admittedly small surveys, one of 500 Americans and the second of 580 Brits with tatts. In both studies, as many as one-third of the subjects reported experiencing buyers' remorse, a reaction most common among men who got their tattoos before turning eighteen.[206]

### . . . to powder your face?

The basic ingredient in most face and body powders is talcum, soft white particles from talc (magnesium silicate, a natural mineral compound comprising magnesium, silicon, and oxygen). Finely ground talc is a super moisture absorbent that smooths surfaces. When used as a face powder, it also helps to even out the color and texture of the skin. But it's important to wield the puff with discretion to avoid shaking loose small particles of talc that may take wing and fly into our mouth and nose, triggering wheezing, coughing and (less commonly) the chronic lung irritation called talcosis.[207]

## . . . to powder your body?

Once you have dried off after a shower or bath (so the powder won't turn into a paste) feel free to powder your feet and your torso, including under your (shaven) arms. If you are female, however, it's important to keep the talc far from your lady parts. Beginning in the 1970s, gynecological researchers began to suspect that powdering the genital area might send talc particles up through the vagina to the uterus and through the fallopian tubes to the ovaries, increasing the risk of ovarian cancer 20-30 percent for women who powder their privates as opposed to those who don't.[208]

## . . . to powder with cornstarch?

If you are sensitive to corn, beware: You may also react to cornstarch. For the non-sensitive, cornstarch—like any powder—is irritating if inhaled. Besides, if you use it as a face powder, you may end up looking like you're wearing a white mask. The good news? It's cheap and unlike talc, there's no link to ovarian cancer.

## . . . to powder the baby?

As long ago as 1969, the New York Poison Control Center was reporting as many as fifty cases of infant talcum aspiration every year. At the time, the American Academy of Pediatrics (AAP) recommended skipping the powder when bathing the baby to avoid his or her breathing in those floating particles.[209] They haven't changed their minds.

## . . . to use deodorant?

There are two kinds of sweat glands, eccrine glands and apocrine glands. The first, found all over the human body, secrete mostly salty water which evaporates quickly. The second, found in hairy spots such as the groin and under the arms, secrete a thicker fluid that turns stinky when it meets the bacteria living naturally on the skin. Deodorants neutralize or mask the odor. Antiperspirants, classified as over-the-counter (OTC) drugs by the Food and

Drug Administration, often contain aluminum compounds such
as aluminum chlorohydrate that
plug the sweat glands and keep
sweat from leaking onto the skin.
Deodorants and antiperspirants
are generally considered both
safe and effective, with two basic
caveats. First, some ingredients
such as the alcohol used to dissolve everything else in the product and the parabens sometimes
included as preservatives may dry

or irritate sensitive skin. Second, there is always the potential for
an allergic reaction, the leading villain being perfume. The Old
Wives' natural alternative is plain baking soda, which neutralizes
odor molecules and blots up excess sweat.[210] Caution: Women preparing for a mammogram must avoid antiperspirants because the
aluminum particles will show up on the X-ray.

### . . . to dry clean your clothes?

"Dry" cleaning isn't dry. It simply uses a solvent rather than soap
and water to clean your clothes. The most common solvent used
to dry clean American clothes is tetrachloroethylene, a.k.a. per-
chloroethylene. PERC, for short, is a probable human carcinogen and a central nervous system depressant that may also affect
color vision and definitely irritates the skin. As a result, the United
States, France, and Denmark banned the use of PERC in buildings
located close to or inside residential structures as of 2009 for exist-
ing machines; in 2020, the ban will be extended to new machines.
Several states, including California, New Jersey, and New York,
have passed legislation that will eventually ban PERC from all dry
cleaning machines.[211] Until then, to reduce the risks PERC poses for

# Who smells worse?

Men and women perspire in exactly the same ways, in the same spots, producing the same sweat from the same glands. As a rule, the male underarm may stay smellier because it is generally unshaven, so liquid lingers longer under there allowing bacteria time to make it really stinky. Ingredient-wise, there is no meaningful difference between deodorant/antiperspirant products for men and those for women, but the price is likely to differ. Unlike haircuts and dry-cleaning, where a woman is likely to pay more for the same service, this is one time where, for some unexplained reason, men pay more. Does that mean a couple should share a single, cheaper female product? No. Using the same roll-on or stick would transfer his or her bacteria to her or him. Be safe. Buy two.

cleaning workers, the United States National Institute for Occupational Safety and Health (OSHA) and the Canadian government have issued a complex set of requirements for using the chemical.[212] But enough about them . . . what about you? It's true that when you bring your dry-cleaned clothes home and whip off the plastic bag some PERC flows out into the air. Whether it is an amount sufficient to produce ill effects remains a question even for serious environmentalists.[213]

## . . . to wear high heels?

When Neil J. Cronin and his colleagues at the Musculoskeletal Research Program at Griffith University (Queensland, Australia) watched nineteen young women march across a specially constructed track with electrodes on their legs to track muscle movements, they saw that women who usually wear high heels walk differently than do women who usually wear flat shoes. Those who customarily wore high heels kept their toes flexed and walked with shorter, more forceful strides than the ladies who usually wore flats. To no one's surprise, this

## Leonardo, Catherine, Louis, and Marie

"The first slim, and shapely high heel may have been the one Leonardo da Vinci made in 1553 as a wedding gift for Catherine of Medici who, according to *Dance Magazine,* needed the extra 2 inches to compete with her future husband's taller mistress. After that, as the art of the period shows, both men and women wore high heels, although with some restrictions such as Louis XIV's rule during his reign from 1643 to 1715, that no one could wear shoes with heels higher than his and that only the nobility could wear them in red. . . . the no-wear rule did not survive the King. On June 12, 1793 Marie Antoinette, proud to the end, rode to the guillotine in an open cart, wearing, some say, 2-inch heels. A few contemporary paintings and engravings do show the heeled shoes; others, have a skirt long enough to hide her feet. . . . her shoes were either thrown away or thrown into the coffin with the queen and buried in an unmarked grave in a small Paris churchyard, where she lay until 1815 when the coffin was dug up and the body reburied at the St. Denis Cathedral with the rest of the royals, executed and otherwise."[215]

shortened the fibers in their calf muscles and put more stress on the muscles. Subsequently, it took more energy for the high-heelers to walk the same distance as women in flats, exhausted their muscles, and increased the risk of injury when they altered the position of their legs and feet when switching to flat sneakers for a workout or long walk.[214] The researchers offered no insight into how often women wearing stilettos are likely to fall out of their shoes.

## . . . to wear flip-flops?

No arch support, no shock absorbers, no cover for your toes which have to grip the shoes to hold them on? Sounds like that could lead to aching arches, ankles, legs, hips, or lower back. Not to mention irritated skin from the strap between your toes, a new risk of skin cancer on your unprotected, un-sunscreened, sometimes-stubbed or stepped-on toes, and walking practically barefoot into unpleasant things.

Merriam-Webster defines kinesiology as "the study of the principles of mechanics and anatomy in relation to human movement." Researchers at Auburn University's College of Education define it in relation to flip-flops as the effects listed above plus a shorter stride that twists your ankle to a larger-than-normal angle as you try to hold the shoes on with your toes. No, you don't have to toss the flip-flops. Just use them sensibly at the beach to avoid sand in

## Stop the Music, Hold the Knife

It's so common for surgeons to play music while working in the operating room that nobody seems to have measured its effect on their performance. In 2016, researchers at London's Centre for Performance Science, Royal College of Music and the Faculty of Medicine, Imperial College London, sort of did. They played Australian rock music while ordinary folk pretended to be doctors at Operation, a board game with moves named after surgical procedures. With rock running in the background, male (but not female) players were much less successful at the game, taking longer to "operate" and making more than the normal number of mistakes. Their conclusion: "Rock music (specifically Australian rock music) appears to have detrimental effects on surgical performance. Men are advised not to listen to rock music when either operating or playing board games."[225]

your other shoes, to keep from tracking water around when you step out of the shower, or just for relaxation.[216]

## . . . to wear a bra?

The notion that wearing a bra may cause breast cancer is an urban myth that has been circulating for decades. It gained added traction in 1995 when a husband-and-wife team of anthropologists published a book called *Dressed to Kill* in which they theorized that bras with underwire increased the risk by trapping toxins in breast tissue. Wasn't true then. Isn't true now.[217]

# Music & Art
# & TV & Books &
# Travel & Weather
# & Paper & Pencils
# & Everything Else

"Life is a banquet, and most poor suckers are starving."

—Edward Everett Tanner III/"Patrick Dennis," *Auntie Mame*

### Is it safe to watch TV?

Forget all those snide comments about what watching television does to your intelligent brain. Instead, check out this June 2014 *USA Today* headline: "Study: Watching Too Much TV Could Lead to Early Death." Then track down the actual report on the actual study that ran in the actual *Journal of the American Heart Association*. No, the study is not about nuclear rays shooting out of the screen to zap you. It's about how much time you spend sitting rather than standing, walking, running, and generally moving about. For eight years, researchers at the University of Navarra (Spain) followed more than thirteen thousand Spanish university

graduates to evaluate the link between sedentary activity—watching TV, using a computer, driving a car—and the risk of premature death. You might think driving would come in first. It didn't. After adjusting for age, gender, smoking status, diet, body mass index, and physical activity, the single significant link to 97 deaths in the group from cardiovascular disease, cancer, and assorted illnesses was time spent watching TV. The risk was "twofold higher for participants reporting ≥3 h/day of television viewing than for those reporting <1 h/day." Multiple previous studies have linked "the sitting disease" (a sedentary lifestyle) to diabetes or heart disease, usually in older people. What makes the Spanish study special is its younger population whose average age was in the mid-30s. "Our findings," the Spanish scientists say, "suggest adults may consider increasing their physical activity, avoid long sedentary periods and reduce television watching to no longer than one to two hours each day."[218]

### . . . to use earphones?

Noise-induced hearing loss (NIHL) is a condition resulting from exposure to very loud sounds for long periods of time, resulting in the injury or destruction of sensory cells inside the ear.[219] The easiest way to prevent or at least reduce the risk of NIHL is simply to

# Can You Hear Me Now?[223]

How loud is *loud* and how long is *long*? The first is measured in decibels (dB). The second may range from seconds to hours. For example, the sound of calm breathing is a 10 dB murmur you can listen to safely forever. An airplane taking off hits 180 dB, 95 dB higher than the 85 dB generally considered safe for human ears (That's about the noise you would hear, when holding a hairdryer 6 inches from your ear) and 70 dB higher than the 110 dB of a chain saw that will make yours hurt within about eight minutes. The following chart ranks familiar sounds by decibel.

| | | | | |
|---|---|---|---|---|
| Airplane take-off | (180 dB) | Vacuum cleaner | (80 dB) |
| Fireworks exploding | (140 dB) | City traffic | (80 dB) |
| Snowmobile motor on | (120 dB) | Normal conversation | (60 dB) |
| Chainsaw on | (110 dB) | Refrigerator humming | (40 dB) |
| Amplified music | (110 dB) | Whisper | (20 dB) |
| Lawn mower | (90 dB) | Leaves rustling | (10 dB) |
| Noisy office | (90 dB) | Calm breathing | (10 dB) |

turn down the volume when you can. Neighbor using a chain saw? Close your window. Listening to your really high-end stereo which is making really high end noise? Dial it down. Listening through earphones? Cleveland Clinic audiologist Sharon A. Sandridge says one stratagem is to balance volume with listening time. "Eighty percent volume for a maximum of 90 minutes is the general rule of thumb," she says. Or you can follow the 60/60 rule: Listen at 60 percent volume for about an hour at a time and then give your ears a break.[220] This is particularly important for children and young adults who sometimes seem to have earphones or ear buds glued permanently in place, perhaps a direct cause of the increased incidence of hearing loss among younger Americans. In 2010 and 2011, data from hearing tests of more than 4,000 adolescents age 12-19, part of the National Health and Nutrition Examination Surveys, found that as exposure to loud noise or music through headphones or ear buds went up from 19.8 percent in 1988-1994 to 34.8 percent in 2005-2006, as did noise-induced threshold shift (NTIs), or the inability to hear sound below a certain level. For no apparent reason, the increase appeared to affect girls rather than boys, raising the level of hearing loss among the former to the level previously seen among the latter.[221] Earbuds and earphones have been around for years so why the newish link to hearing loss? The answers seem to be technology, ear buds that deliver sound directly into the ear at levels that may rise to more than 100 decibels, a level safe for less than three minutes, and devices that store literally thousands of songs permitting an uninterrupted listening time that may extend for hours. How to tell if the noise is too loud? Jim Battey, the director of the National Institute on Deafness and Other Communication Disorders, says that if you are an arm's length away, the person wearing headphones or earbuds should be able to hear what you say. If they can't, "that level of noise is unsafe and potentially damaging."[222]

## . . . to play computer games?

The web site www.spike.com has actually compiled a list of "The Top 10 Deaths Caused by Video Games," beginning with the Korean gentleman known only as Lee, who collapsed due to "heart failure stemming from exhaustion" in 2005 while playing Starcraft and working up to Alabama teenager Devin Darnell Thompson (a.k.a. Devin Moore). As spike.com describes it, on June 7, 2003, Thompson/Moore, a Grand Theft Auto (GTA) addict, "took one gun from an officer, shot three others with it, and fled the station in a police cruiser. Moore was obsessed with the GTA series of video games, and, once captured, he told police 'Life's like a video game.

You've got to die sometime.'" Which day remains to be seen. Thompson was sentenced to death in 2005; the sentence was upheld in 2012; and as of this writing he remains on death row.[224]

## . . . to write a book?

It depends on when you live, where you live, and what you have to say. Wikipedia, the source of all information past, present, and future, has a clickable list of fifty-one executed writers most of whom who went to their deaths because of what they thought and wrote.[226] They range from the ancient (Cicero) to the famous (Isaac Babel, Andre Chenier, Federico Garcia Lorca, Thomas More, Sir Walter Raleigh[227]) and to some of whom you have almost certainly never heard such as Hu Yepin (1903-1931), one of the "Five Martyrs of the Left League" executed by Chiang Kai-Shek's Kuomintang government. Not all executed writers were heroes, of course. Some were simply criminally unpleasant like twenty-seven-year-old Jacques Fesch (1930-1957), who was guillotined in Paris for having killed a policeman during a robbery but whose book about his conversion to devout Catholicism while in prison awaiting execution was deemed so powerful that he has been proposed for beatification.[228]

## . . . to read a book?

You might want to watch out for political polemics or books that insult your intelligence by promoting the twenty-first century version of "the earth is flat" or tell you to lose weight by living on air.[229] Or you could join the American Library Association in celebrating literary freedom during its

## Reading Really Dirty Books

In 2013, two Belgian researchers tested books in the Antwerp Library for germs. What they found was traces of the herpes virus on borrowed copies of the popular *Fifty Shades of Grey* The viral concentrations weren't high enough to be hazardous to readers' health, but there was this second complication: The books also tested positive for cocaine.[232]

annual Banned Book Week because, as Stephen King once wrote, "Books are a uniquely portable magic."

## . . . to read a library book?

Libraries may look neat and clean, but every day their books are handled by more people than you can count on all of your fingers and toes and every other body part combined. So you'd expect those books to be more contagious than your own. You'd probably be wrong. In 1994, when researchers from the C. E. Smith Jewish Day School in Rockville, Maryland, and the Department of Pediatrics at Georgetown University School of Medicine counted the microbes on fifteen library books and fifteen books from private homes, they found the same relatively small number of *Staphylococcus epidermidis* (a microbe normally resident on human skin) on the same number of volumes in both collections.[230] Seventeen years later, when students at Brigham Young University (Utah) ran a similar study, this time to rank the cleanliness of their library as well as its books, they found pretty much the same result. True, the more popular had up to 45 percent more microbe colonies than the less circulated books, but the really disgustingly bug-laden things in the building were the doorknobs.[231]

## . . . to fly First Class?

Free champagne, caviar, a goodie-bag, flat bed, showers, maybe even a cabin to yourself, what could be classier than First Class?

Surviving a crash. If that's your true test of classy, First Class may not be your best bet. After analyzing seating charts from seventeen crashes, the first in 1985, the last in 2000, *Time Magazine* announced in 2015 that the safest place to be when things go wrong is a middle seat in a crowded row far back in Economy Land where the fatality rate in a crash was about 28 percent. The un-safest seats were on the aisle in the middle of the plane, in the Business Class cabin, where the fatality rate was 16 points higher. In reality, the FAA and other airline safety experts say there is no "safest" seat because in the event of an accident, who lives and who dies is pretty much random, depending on how the plane goes down. If the tail hits hardest, people in the back are not likely to survive no matter where they sit. It's reality as well to note that flying a commercial airline is safer than lots of other means of transportation. Your lifetime odds of leaving this life in a car crash are 1 in 112; getting hit by that car while a pedestrian, 1 in 672; on a motorbike, 1 in 948. On a plane, the odds go way down to just 1 in 8,000. Now that's classy.[233]

### . . . to stay seated to during the flight?

Ordinarily, it's best to stay seated and buckled up to avoid bouncing if the plane hits turbulence, but there's an exception to every rule. While flying, you may be at risk of developing deep vein thrombosis (DVT), blood clots in your leg due to staying cramped in a small space, i.e. the newest seats on an airplane, which in some cases have as little as 28 inches of leg room between yours and the one in front of you. To reduce the risk, Mount Sinai (New York) cardiologist Allen Stewart advises you to stay hydrated and while seated, flex your calf muscles frequently to keep blood moving smoothly, then get up and walk around from time to time. Given the shrinking room that may make it difficult to edge your way past the passenger next to you, consider opting for an aisle seat rather than the one with the view through the window.[234]

### . . . to ride in the first car on a train?

Every year, an average of nine hundred Americans die in a train crash, but not necessarily because the train crashed. The biggest problem is drivers and pedestrians who ignore the warnings at grade crossings sometimes, it seems, to commit suicide by train. The same is true of subways. In 2013, fifty-three people died when they jumped, fell, or were pushed onto the tracks at one of the New York City subway's 472 stations.[235] Across the country, on San Francisco's forty-four-station BART system, there were five such deaths, enough to prompt an expansion of suicide prevention services in the under/over-ground system.[236] Take careless drivers, pedestrians, and riders out of the equation and the actual fatality rate on American railroads is 0.15 people per billion passenger miles.[237] Urban mythology says the unfortunate 0.15 person was sitting in the first car or the last, the two most likely to be hit in a head-on smash-up. However, modern trains are more likely to derail than to hit each other. In the ten year period from 2005 to 2014, the Federal Railroad Administration (FRA) counted about 13,000 derailments vs. about 1,500 collisions. When a train derails, cars may be upended or crushed. Ross Capon, former president of the National Association of Railroad passengers, says that if that happens, aisle seats are safer than seats next to windows where a passenger is more likely to be cut by broken glass or be thrown from the car. A rear-facing seat is also safer, because a person sitting there is less likely to be thrown forward during a collision. Café cars are dangerous because their hard high tables can slam into passengers at chest level if the train comes to a sudden stop.[238] Nonetheless, if your pleasure on a subway is to stand at the front of the first car, looking out the little window as the train rolls on, and the signal lights blink and change, go for it.

## . . . is it safe to fly at zero G?

We've all seen pictures of astronauts floating in a no-gravity cabin, and most people know that not having to fight the pull of gravity disorients your proprioceptive system, the brain function

# Birth Order Rules

"Who's in the middle?" Most children and adults hate the middle seat with its awkward bump on the floor and bodies pressed against you on either side. But who ends up sitting there when the family goes for a drive may owe much to who's oldest and who's not. When University of Buffalo researchers studied crash-related fatalities, the best survival bet in the back was the seat in the middle. Overall, in the Buffalo study, the average age of backseat passengers was twenty. But the average age of the person in the middle was only a few months past fifteen. In other words, the older sibling gets the apparent "win" (the window seat), but the younger sibling gets the safer middle.[243]

that tells you what's up and where's down and lets you know where your limbs are. As one Apollo astronaut told a NASA interviewer, "The first night in space when I was drifting off to sleep, I suddenly realized that I had lost track of my arms and legs. For all my mind could tell, my limbs were not there."[239] The lack of gravity also weakens bones, which lose calcium, and shrinks muscles that lack proper resistance exercise. Thanks to astronaut brothers Scott and Mark Kelly, NASA now knows that there are changes in the body on a cellular level as well. The Kelly boys aren't just brothers, they're research gold: identical twins who agreed to be part of a study of how living gravity-free affects the human body. From March 27, 2015 to March 1, 2016, Scott spent 340 consecutive days aboard the International Space Station (ISS). Once he returned to Earth, NASA scientists were able to compare his body with that of his twin. What they discovered was that Scott's telomeres grew slightly longer while he was in space, but returned to normal shortly after he got back. On the other hand, Mark's telomeres behaved normally, shortening during the year.[240] Telomeres are short chains of organic molecules called nucleotides that protect the ends of chromosomes. Normally, telomere shortening is an age-related process. In some cells, such as those in your bones and muscles, the telomeres get shorter every time the cell replicates itself, and eventually the cell dies. Other cells, such as blood stem cells in your bone marrow, are constantly reproducing an enzyme called telomerase that rebuilds the telomeres so the cells can keep up the job. The good news is that you have a continuing supply of new blood cells. The bad news is that cancer cells also seem to have the ability to activate telomerase, which allows them to keep dividing indefinitely. Some previous studies have found an association between short telomeres and high mortality, including an increased risk of dying from cancer. Others haven't.[241] The NASA studies may add to the mix.

### . . . to sit in the passenger seat?

Once upon a time, not so long ago, the passenger seat in an automobile was commonly known as "the death seat." Today, advances in car safety such as seat belts and air bags designed to absorb the impact in a crash have made the front seat safer. Now the problem is the back seat, says Jessica Jermakian, a senior research scientist at the Insurance Institute for Highway Safety (IIHS). It's still the safest place for children and child car seats, but that's not the case for adults, perhaps because adults riding in the back seat don't think they have to buckle up.[242]

### . . . to turn right on red?

If you live in the western United States, you've been doing this for more than fifty years. Easterners got their chance when the Federal Energy Policy and Conservation Act of 1975 required states to put red-light-turn regulations in place in order to conserve fuel which would otherwise be wasted as engines idled waiting to turn. Naturally, the new laws came with some restrictions. For example, Maine allows you to turn right turn on red—but not if there's a pedestrian or bicyclist crossing in front of you or a sign saying you can't.[244] In New York City, you can't unless the sign says you can. In California, a red arrow means no turns, left or right. Drive north into Canada, and you can turn right on red after a complete stop so long as there's no "no" sign, except in Montreal where you can't, no matter what. Ditto if you head south into Mexico and Mexico City. In China, you can turn right on red, but not on a red arrow. In Japan, which drives on the left, you can turn left on red if there's a green arrow pointing left. In the United States, five— Alaska, Idaho, Michigan, Oregon, and Washington—permit left turns on red onto a one-way street even from a two-way street. The safe rule: Learn before you turn.

### . . . to ride a motorcycle?

Your lifetime risk of dying while riding on a motorcycle is 1 in 948 which is less than your risk of dying in a car crash (1 in 113) but higher than while riding a plain pedal bicycle (1 in 4,337).[245]

### . . . to cross the street?

With both cars and bicycles whizzing by, the classic advice to "cross at the green, not in-between" may not be enough to get you from one side to the other in one piece, especially if you own a cell phone. It's currently illegal in many places to use a cell while driving, but it's still legal to stare at the phone while walking, and multiple studies show pedestrians do it all the time. In 2013, a University of Georgia study found that 26 percent of pedestrians wore headphones, 15 percent were texting, and 13 percent talked on the phone at high risk intersections. Two years later, a similar study at William Paterson University (New Jersey) found more than a quarter of all New York City pedestrians distracted by either their phones or headphones.[246] The results are predictable. In 2013, 6,100 pedestrians were killed by motor vehicles; 160,000 survived but suffered injuries serious enough to require medical attention, meaning we now count one pedestrian death every two hours in the United States.[247] The better way? As Philadelphia elected officials say, "Put. Phone. Down."[248]

## . . . to take the lift?

Every year in the United States, elevators go up and down more than eighteen billion times. In the process, mechanical failure and/ or human error lead to an average of twenty-six or twenty-seven fatalities. As the astute mathematicians at the *Los Angeles Times* discovered, that means your risk of dying on one of those trips in the lift is 0.00000015 percent. The folks most at risk are the ones who install and service the elevators. They total to approximately fourteen deaths in elevator accidents a year vs. six for people using an elevator at work and another six for people riding the lift while not at work. In other words, if you are not an elevator worker, your own risk of an elevator death can pretty much be described as infinitesimal.

## . . . to walk the stairs?

Walking up and down stairs is a relatively good form of exercise. Twenty minutes six or seven times a week comes close to meeting the Centers for Disease Control and Prevention's recommendation that adults do at least 150 minutes of moderate-intensity cardio-beneficial exercise a week.[249] The walk builds muscles in your calves and thighs and burns a respectable amount of calories, approximately 180 for every twenty-minute trek up or down or up and down. Some even feel energetic enough to jog up and down, increasing the exercise impact and burning even more calories, but running on stairs is not for amateurs. The National Safety Council estimates that 210,640 Americans died in 2000 after falling on stairs; your own lifetime risk of ending up on that list is 1 in 2,739. Falls are most common among the very young and the older. Seniors account for about 70 percent of the adult slips; experts at the Center for Injury Research and Policy at Nationwide Children's Hospital (Columbus, Ohio) found that every six minutes an American child is treated in an Emergency Room for an injury resulting from a fall on the stairs, usually in his own home.[250] To reduce the risk of falling, sometimes with fatal consequences, the Public Health Agency of Canada has drawn up "12 Rules for Stair Safety." To wit:

1. Install lights and switches to ensure all your stairways are well lit.
2. Make sure there are no uneven surfaces, cracks, bunched-up stair-covering, or protruding nails.
3. Have a carpenter correct uneven steps. They are a major hazard.
4. Paint a contrasting color on the edge of wooden or concrete steps (or on the top and bottom steps), or apply special strips you can buy to enhance the visibility of each step.
5. Stair carpeting can cause slips. Consider removing it or replacing it with well-secured rubber stair treading.
6. Make sure the handrail is well-secured and that you can get your full hand around it.
7. There should be a handrail on at least one side of all stairways. The height should allow you to use it comfortably when your arm is slightly bent at the elbow.
8. Avoid storing things temporarily on your stairs. Always check the stairs as you walk up or down.
9. Loose floor coverings are a hazard. If you have rugs make sure they are non-slip, or have a rubber backing.
10. Go slowly with your hand on the handrail. Rushing is a major cause of falls.
11. If you're carrying something, make sure it doesn't hide the stairs and that one hand is free to use the handrail.
12. Be sure to remove your reading glasses when walking or climbing up or down stairs. If you use bifocals, adjust your glasses so you can see the stairs clearly.[251]

### . . . to hold the handrail?

Holding the handrail when you walk down a flight of stairs provides extra stability and insurance against tripping, but in infectious disease talk, the word "handrail" is practically a synonym for "third rail." As you reach for the one on a public stairway or escalator, consider how many naked hands have touched it before yours. On a cruise ship where you worry about the notorious norovirus, consider that the villainous microbe is easily transmitted by a carrier/victim's touching something such as a deck chair, a water faucet, or the handrails on the gangplank, on the stairways, or on the edge of the deck. Of course, on land or sea, the best defense is the simplest one: Wash your hands after touching the handrail.[252]

### . . . to push a shopping cart?

Charles Gerba, a University of Arizona microbiologist who spends a lot of time studying germs in public places, wants you to know that up to eight of every ten shopping carts nationwide may have *E. coli* or salmonella and *campylobacter* on their handles, deposited there by people who picked up leaking packages of raw meat and poultry and then reached to push the cart. Handling fruits and veggies may also produce problems. Most supermarkets sprinkle the produce with water to keep it fresh, but dampness promotes mold and, in addition, spraying may contaminate the plant foods with *Legionella*, the respiratory disease bacteria that lurks in water systems everywhere.[253] And what about the straps on seats that let you put your infant safely in the cart?

True, they will keep him from falling out, but like infant seats in restaurant, literally dozens, maybe hundreds of kids have sneezed or drooled on them before you belted yours in place.

## . . . to watch the storm through a window?

Is the window open or closed? If it's open, and you're standing on or near something that conducts electricity—perhaps a floor made of concrete which sometimes has metal bars imbedded to make it stronger—yes, the lightning could hit that and you. If the window's framed in metal rather than wood, ditto. If the window is closed and lightning hits the glass, it will explode the pane which might send pieces of glass flying here and there and maybe into you.

## . . . to use a phone during a thunderstorm?

Do you worry that lightning will hit the telephone cable, buried or above ground, and zap though it into you? Yes, there was one such incident in New Jersey in 1985, another in New York in 1988, and eighteen years later, in 2006, a sixty-four-year-old Mississippian went to his reward when lightning hit his phone. But from 2007 to 2015, the last year for which there are statistics, the National Weather Service (NWS) website reports no, nada, zero such deaths by telephone in the United States.[254] Nonetheless, in an excess of caution, NWS does suggest you "stay off corded phones, computers and other electrical equipment that put you in direct contact with electricity" while the storm is raging.[255] The important word there, of course, is the

modifier, "corded." According to SNOPES, the quirky site that tracks and de-mythifies misinformation, "cell phones (and cordless portable phones) used indoors during electrical storms are perfectly safe because there is no wire through which the electrical discharge could travel.[256] As for simply carrying a cell phone while you're outside, when a British medical journal published a report from a group of doctors who insisted that doing so was dangerous, University of Florida lightning expert Vladimir Rakov shot it down: "I don't think that having a cell phone in your pocket can change the outcome of a lightning strike," he said. His best advice? "Don't remain outdoors during a thunderstorm, whether you carry a cell phone or not."[257]

### . . . to use a cell phone?

Radiation causes cancer. Cell phones emit radiation. Therefore, holding a cell next to your head increases your risk of brain cancer, right? Wrong. It's true that exposure to ionizing radiation such as X-rays disrupts DNA in your body cells, increasing your risk of cancer, but cell phones emit radiofrequency energy, a.k.a. "radio waves," which does not damage DNA. In 2016, preliminary results of a National Institute of Environmental Health Sciences (NIEHS) study showed no clear evidence of a link between cell phones and brain cancer. This echoes the results or several other large scale surveys such as the European 13-country, 358,000-person Interphone study,[258] the United States Million Women Study, and the NCI Surveillance, Epidemiology, and End Results (SEER) Program. Yes, a few studies have suggested a statistical link between cell phones and cancer, but epidemiology doesn't support that. The number of American cell phone users has grown exponentially from about one hundred million in 2000 to more than three hundred million in 2014, yet the incidence of brain cancer has not gone up. Researchers suggest that data from studies linking cell phones to brain cancer may be due to recall bias (a failure to remember exact details about cell phone use), or participation bias (studies enrolling more people with brain cancer than those without). In addition, advances in technology have made it possible to lower the energy required to work the phone. Nonetheless, some experts remain cautious. In 2011, citing limited evidence from human studies and the theoretical risk to children, a World Health Organization (WHO) Working Group classified cell phones as "possibly carcinogenic to humans," and the Food and Drug Administration suggests using your cell for short conversations during which you hold it away from your head or use a "hands free" device.[259]

### . . . to use a cell phone on a plane?

In 1991, when cell phones were barely a blip

## Listen to this

Like cell phones, perhaps earphones should be verboten while walking. Each type comes with good news and bad. For example, over-the-ear headphones cover the entire ear. The good news is that they give you better sound at lower decibels and because they don't go inside your ear, so while wearing them you may be able to hear what's happening around you. The bad news is that every action has an equal and opposite reaction: You're likely to step up the volume to block that extra noise which defeats the good news. The same applies to earbuds. Isolating earbuds fit tightly into your ears so you can listen at lower volume. That's the good news. The bad news is that these tight-fitting, rubber-based plugs can prevent you from hearing warning sounds such as the bike coming up on the sidewalk behind you or the car speeding through the intersection your crossing.

on the communications scene, the Federal Communications Commission (FCC) banned their use on airplanes. That left travelers either fuming at being cut off from the world and/or fearful that if they turned on the phone the plane would crash. Well, no. Contrary to common wisdom, the cell phone would not have interfered with either the plane's electrical systems or transmissions to and from the cockpit, but their signals might have messed up communications back on earth as every phone on the plane bounced around wireless networks on the ground. In 2014, the FCC changed its mind, giving airlines the right to decide whether to permit cell phone use on their flights. But you can't please everyone. One year before the ban was lifted, a Quinnipiac University poll in 2013 found that only 30 percent of adults surveyed favored removing it. It surprised a lot of people to learn that a solid majority of tech-savvy respondents age eighteen to twenty-nine agreed. More than half (52 percent) were opposed to enabling phones on planes.[260]

### . . . to use a cell phone while driving a car?
No.

### . . . to use headphones while driving a car?
No.

### . . . to look at your computer screen?
Like television screens, computer screens flicker—a problem for people with certain vision deficits or for those with epilepsy. To help you choose the least troublesome monitor, the British organization Epilepsy Action describes the screens according to their flicker potential. The screens most likely to flicker are on older cathode ray tube (CRT) monitors. Liquid crystal display (LCD) screens such as light-emitting diode (LED) and thin-filament tran-

sistor (TFT-LCD) screens flicker much less, but their bright colors may be irritating. The same goes for plasma display panel (PDP) screens.[261]

## . . . to chew your pencil?

It may give your dentist agita, particularly if you're wearing braces or pricey porcelain veneers, but contrary to common wisdom chewing your pencil won't give you lead poisoning because pencils aren't now and never have been made with lead. Right from the beginning, that dark stuff in the center has been harmless graphite and clay. Thanks to modern government regulation there's no lead in the paint on the shaft, either.[262]

## . . . to pick up a piece of paper?

Like your lips, feet, and toes, your fingertips are packed with sensory nerves and pain receptors. The edges of a piece of paper are sharp enough to slice through the skin on your finger tip. If you hit the paper at the wrong angle, you will definitely know it.

## Brain Pain, Not

Your brain is the organ that enables you to collect and translate sensory messages from the nerves throughout your body. For example, when you touch something, it's your brain—not your finger—that that says "rough" or "smooth" or "hot" or "cold" or "ouch!" Touching actual brain tissue delivers no such messages because the brain has no translators of its own. The scalp and the meninges (tissues that cover the brain) do, but once they are anesthetized, surgeons can perform "wide awake brain surgery," cutting into brain tissue without causing discomfort. This allows the patient and surgeon to communicate during the procedure, a highly protective situation that helps avoid accidental damage to vital functions. For example, during surgery, to remove a tumor in an area that might affect speech, the doctor can ask the patient to talk, thus confirming that this sense remains intact.[263]

# APPENDIX

## Calculate Your Risk

Your risk of dying is 100 percent. Your risk of dying from whatever carries off your relatives, friends, and neighbors? Not necessarily the same as theirs. Everyone dies, but not everyone dies of the same thing, so the National Safety Council has compiled a selected list of some of the more common ways in which living a perfectly ordinary American life can do you in.[264] Your actual personal odds may vary with various factors, most specifically your gender, your genes, and your geography. For example, in the United States, men are more likely than women to die by suicide or in an auto accident, and in 2014, the Centers for Disease Control and Prevention found rural Americans at higher risk than urbanites of death by heart disease, stroke, cancer, chronic respiratory diseases, and accidental injuries, due in part, perhaps, to more smoking, more guns, and fewer seat belts. Unfortunately, neither the Centers for Disease Control and Prevention nor the National Safety Council have released a statistical prediction of the odds of your dying from hiding in your room with the doors and windows locked to avoid every other risk.

## Cause of Death Lifetime Odds of Dying from This

Being Human. . . . . . . . . . . . . . . . . . . . . . . . . . . . . 1 in 1
Heart Disease and Cancer . . . . . . . . . . . . . . . . . . . . 1 in 7
Chronic Lower Respiratory Disease . . . . . . . . . . . . 1 in 27
Intentional Self-Harm (Suicide) . . . . . . . . . . . . . . . 1 in 97
Unintentional Poisoning by and Exposure
to Noxious Substances . . . . . . . . . . . . . . . . . . . . . 1 in 103

Motor Vehicle Crash . . . . . . . . . . . . . . . . . . . . . 1 in 113
Fall. . . . . . . . . . . . . . . . . . . . . . . . . . . . . . . . . . . 1 in 133
Assault by Firearm . . . . . . . . . . . . . . . . . . . . . 1 in 358
Pedestrian Incident. . . . . . . . . . . . . . . . . . . . . 1 in 672
Motorcycle Rider Incident . . . . . . . . . . . . . . . 1 in 948
Unintentional Drowning and Submersion . . . . . 1 in 1,183
Exposure to Fire, Flames, or Smoke . . . . . . . . . 1 in 1,454
Choking on Your Food. . . . . . . . . . . . . . . . . . . 1 in 3,408
Pedal Cyclist Incident. . . . . . . . . . . . . . . . . . . . 1 in 4,337
Firearms Discharge (accidental) . . . . . . . . . . . . 1 in 7,944
Air and Space Transport Incidents
(Plane crash). . . . . . . . . . . . . . . . . . . . . . . . . . . 1 in 9,737
Exposure to Excessive Natural Heat
(Heatstroke). . . . . . . . . . . . . . . . . . . . . . . . . . . 1 in 10,784
Exposure to Electric Current, Radiation,
Temperature, and Pressure . . . . . . . . . . . . . . . . 1 in 14,695
Contact with Sharp Objects . . . . . . . . . . . . . . . 1 in 30,860
Cataclysmic Storm . . . . . . . . . . . . . . . . . . . . . . 1 in 63,679
Contact with Hornets, Wasps, and Bees . . . . . . 1 in 64,706
Contact with Heat and Hot Substances . . . . . . 1 in 69,169
Legal Execution . . . . . . . . . . . . . . . . . . . . . . . . 1 in 111,439
Being Bitten or Struck by a Dog. . . . . . . . . . . . 1 in 114,622
Lightning Strike. . . . . . . . . . . . . . . . . . . . . . . . 1 in 174,426

# END NOTES

All websites referenced in these notes
were accessed April 2016–May 2017.

# 1
# Animals

1. "Five To One," *Waiting for the Sun* (1968)
   John Densmore, Jim Morris, Robbie Kreiger, Ray Manzarek.
   *"No one here gets out alive, now,*
   *You get yours, baby,*
   *I'll get mine,*
   *Gonna make it, baby"*
2. Colleen Cappon, "Is it Safe to Kiss Your Pet?," *Fox News,* March 11,
   2011, http://www.foxnews.com/health/2011/03/11/safe-kiss-pet.html.
3. James P. Wilson, Kalman Kafetz, and Douglas Fink, "Case Report: Lick
   of Death: Capnocytophaga canimorsus is an Important Cause of Sepsis in the Elderly." *BMJ Case Reports 2016,* June 30, 2016, http://casere-
   ports.bmj.com/content/2016/bcr-2016-215450.abstract.
4. Jeffrey Barret and John L. Brusch, "Human Bites," *Medscape,* http://
   emedicine.medscape.com/article/218901-overview.
5. "Man Dies After He Gets Bitten by his Pet Cat," AOL, July 1, 2016,
   http://www.aol.com/article/2016/07/01/man-dies-after-he-gets-bitten-
   by-his-pet-cat/21422861/.
6. Christina Nelson, Shubhayu Saha, and Paul Mead, "Cat Scratch Disease
   in the United States, 2005–2013," *Emerging Infectious Disease,* October
   2016, 22 (10), http://wwwnc.cdc.gov/eid/article/22/10/16-0115_article.

7       "Parasites—Toxoplasmosis (Toxoplasma infection) Epidemiology and
        Risk Factors," *Centers for Disease Control and Prevention,* http://www.
        cdc.gov/parasites/toxoplasmosis/epi.html.

8.      Allison Kim Perry, "How to safely clean a cat's litter box," *Animal
        Planet,* http://www.animalplanet.com/pets/how-to-safely-clean-cat-
        ltter-box/.

9.      Steven Pro, "Micobacterium marinum: The Fish Disease You Could
        Catch," *Reefkeeping,* April 2009, 8 (3), http://reefkeeping.com/
        issues/2003–07/sp/feature/index.htm; "Mycobacterium marinum
        Fact Sheet," *Provet Healthcare Information,* updated October 2013,
        http://www.provet.co.uk/health/diseases/mycobacteriummarinum.
        htm; Bob Fenner, "It's Just A Scratch; Or Is It? Wound Management,
        Livestock Toxicity and Pet Fishing," *Wet Web Media,* n.d., http://
        www.wetwebmedia.com/Wound.htm.

10.     "Warnings: Some Cats Never Grow Out of Hunting the Fish They
        Live With," *WikiHow,* http://www.wikihow.com/Keep-Fish-when-
        You-Have-Cats-That-Like-to-Hunt.

11.     Other pet animals such as chicks, ducklings, and small rodents (think
        hamsters) may also harbor *Salmonella* bacteria.

12.     LA County, *Ibid.*

13.     "Four Multistate Outbreaks of Human Salmonella Infections Linked
        to Small Turtles," *Centers for Disease Control and Prevention,* May
        18, 2016, http://www.cdc.gov/salmonella/small-turtles-10-15/index.
        html.

14.     Karen Kaplan, "Parasitologist Bestows Squirmy Honor on his Distant
        Cousin, President Obama," *LA Times,* September 8, 2016, http://
        www.latimes.com/science/sciencenow/la-sci-sn-obama-parasitic-
        worm-20160908-snap-story.html.

15.     "Barack Obama is Officially Now a Parasite (It's an Honor)," *Yahoo
        Finance*, n.d., http://finance.yahoo.com/news/barack-obama-officially-
        now-parasite-honor-185458407—politics.html.

16.     David Millward, "Barack Obama is a Parasite—He is Also a Spider
        and an Extinct Lizard, "*The Telegraph News,* September 10, 2016,

http://www.telegraph.co.uk/news/2016/09/10/barack-obama-is-a-parasite—he-is-also-a-spider-and-an-extinct/.

17. Bob Morris, "Warm Nights, Cold Noses," *The New York Times,* February 16, 2011, http://www.nytimes.com/2011/02/17/garden/17pets.html?pagewanted=all&_r=0.

18. "Are Your Pets Disturbing Your Sleep? You're Not Alone, Mayo Clinic Study Finds," *Newswise,* June 3, 2014, http://www.newswise.com/articles/view/618806/?sc=mwtr&xy=5003042.

19. "Babies Should Sleep in Parents' Room, New Guidelines Say," *NBC News*, October 24, 2016, http://www.nbcnews.com/health/kids-health/babies-should-sleep-parents-room-new-guidelines-say-n672011.

20. "She Sleeps With Her Snake Each Night Until Doctors Tell Her This," *Newslinq*, 2016, http://www.newslinq.com/woman-sleeping-with-snake/.

21. Anahad O'Connor, "The Raw Food Diet for Pets," *The New York Times*, May 23, 2012, https://well.blogs.nytimes.com/2012/05/23/the-raw-food-diet-for-pets/.

22. "Pet Obesity on the Rise for Sixth Straight Year," *PR Newswire*, January 4, 2017, http://www.prnewswire.com/news-releases/pet-obesity-on-the-rise-for-sixth-straight-year-300385293.html.

23. "Foods Cats Shouldn't Eat," *WebMD*, Reviewed by Amy Flowers, September 1, 2016, http://pets.webmd.com/ss/slideshow-people-foods-cats-can-eat; "Pets and People: 10 Table Foods Pets Shouldn't Eat, *Animal Planet*, n.d., http://www.animalplanet.com/pets/healthy-pets/table-foods-pets/; "Macadamia Nuts and Dogs Don't Mix," *About,* 2016, http://vetmedicine.about.com/od/f/ToxicMacadamia-Nuts.htm/toxicology.

24. Andy Newman, "Dogs on Marijuana: Not Cool," *The New York Times*, February 2, 2017, https://www.nytimes.com/2017/02/02/nyregion/marijuana-dogs-weed.html.

25. "What Dog Has the Strongest Bite?" *Reference.com*, https://www.reference.com/pets-animals/dog-strongest-bite-f901567da98c56b5?qo=-

contentSimilarQuestions#; "Dangerous Encounters," *National Geographic*, August 8, 2005, http://www.reptilia.org/national-geographics-dr-brady-barrs-bite-pressure-tests/;"Top 20 Strongest Bites in the Animal Kingdom," February 27, 2015, http://imgur.com/gallery/WB4VP.

26. Kassahun T. Jaleta, Sharon Rose Hill, Göran Birgersson, Habte Tekie, and Rickard Ignell, "Chicken Volatiles Repel Host-Seeking Malaria Mosquitoes," *The Malaria Journal*, 2016, 15 (354), http://malariajournal.biomedcentral.com/articles/10.1186/s12936-016-1386-3.

27. Colin Basler, Thai-An Nguyen, Tara C. Anderson, Thane Hancock, and Casey Barton Behravesh, "Outbreaks of Human Salmonella Infections Associated with Live Poultry, United States, 1990–2014," *Centers for Disease Control and Prevention*, http://wwwnc.cdc.gov/eid/article/22/10/15-0765_article.

28. Vance Kawakami, Krista Reitberg, Beth Lipton, Kaye Eckmann, Matyann Watkins, Hanna Oltean, Meagan Kay, Chantal Rothschild, Miwako Kobayashi, Chris Van Beneden, and Jeff Duchin, "Notes from the Field: Fatal Infection Associated with Equine Exposure— King County, Washington," *CDC Morbidity and Mortality Weekly Report*, August 5, 2016, http://www.cdc.gov/mmwr/volumes/65/wr/mm6530a5.htm.

29. Theodore Geisel (Dr. Seuss), *Horton Hears a Who!*, (New York: Random House, 1954).

30. James Ritchie, "Fact or Fiction?: Elephants Never Forget," *Scientific American*, January 12, 2009, https://www.scientificamerican.com/article/elephants-never-forget/.

31. Ismail Azzam, "Girl Killed by Zoo Elephant," *CNN*, July 29, 2016, http://www.cnn.com/2016/07/28/middleeast/elephant-kills-child-morocco/index.html.

32. Ritchie, *Ibid.*

33. Found naturally or widespread among animals, from the Greek prefix *en-* meaning *among* and *zoion* meaning *animal*; similar to *endemic*, from *en-* plus *demos,* meaning *among people*.

# Endnotes

34.     "Rabies Surveillance in the United States during 2014," *Centers for Disease Control and Prevention*, updated April 29, 2016, http://www.cdc.gov/rabies/location/usa/surveillance/index.html.

35.     Lauren F. Friedman, "How a Handful of Americans Got a Terrifying, Extremely Rare Disease from Raccoon Poop," *Business Insider, AOL,* September 6, 2016, http://www.aol.com/article/news/2016/09/08/how-a-handful-of-americans-got-a-terrifying-extremely-rare-dise/21468595/?icid=maing-grid7%7Cmain5%7Cdl13%7Csec1_lnk3%26pLid%3D-199483585_htmlws-main-bb.

36.     "Myth Busting: The Truth About Animals and Tools," *Morning Edition*, December 23, 2011, http://www.npr.org/2011/12/23/143833929/myth-busting-the-truth-about-animals-and-tools.

37.     "What is Dengue Fever?" *Scitable*, 2014, http://www.nature.com/scitable/topicpage/what-is-dengue-fever-22399100.

38.     "Malaria Facts," *Centers for Disease Control and Prevention*, updated April 15, 2016, http://www.cdc.gov/malaria/about/facts.html; "Zika Virus, Transmission and Risks," *Centers for Disease Control and Prevention*, updated August 27, 2016, http://www.cdc.gov/zika/transmission/index.html; "Chikungunya," *WHO*, Updated April 2016, http://www.who.int/mediacentre/factsheets/fs327/en/.

39.     "Injury Facts® 2016 Edition," *National Safety Council*, http://www.nsc.org/learn/safety-knowledge/Pages/injury-facts-chart.aspx.

# 2

# Food

40.     Also known as *Sodium Dichloroisocyanurate, Troclosene Sodium, sodium troclosene, troclosenum natricum* or *SDIC*.

41. "Preventing Travellers' Diarrrhoea: How to Make Drinking Water Safe," *World Health Organization*, May 2007, http://www.who.int/water_sanitation_health/hygiene/envsan/sdwtravel.pdf.

42. "Flint Water Crisis," *Wikipedia,* https://en.wikipedia.org/wiki/Flint_water_crisishttps://en.wikipedia.org/wiki/Flint_water_crisis.

43. Linda K. Leising, Philip L. McCarthy, Jr., Theresa Hahn, Lauren Dunford, and Melissa McKernon, "Bottled Water Myths: Separating Fact from Fiction," *Practical Gastroenterology*, May 2007, http://www.practicalgastro.com/pdf/May07/May07LeisingArticle.pdf.

44. Amanda L. Chan, "What You Need To Know Before You Reuse That Plastic Water Bottle," *Huffington Post,* updated Oct 13, 2014, http://www.huffingtonpost.com/2014/08/14/reuse-plastic-water-bottle_n_5671681.html.

45. Kenneth G. Libbrecht, *"Is It Really True That No Two Snowflakes Are Alike?" Snow Crystals*, n.d., http://www.its.caltech.edu/~atomic/snowcrystals/alike.

46. Anne Marie Helmenstine, "Can You Eat Snow?" *About*, updated January 23, 2016, http://chemistry.about.com/od/waterchemistry/fl/Is-It-Safe-To-Eat-Snow.htm.

47. "Rainwater Is Safe To Drink, Australian Study Suggests," *ScienceDaily*, November 6, 2009, www.sciencedaily.com/releases/2009/11/091104091728.htm.

48. "The History of Food Canning: About Canned Food and Whence It Came," *Reference,* http://www.foodreference.com/html/artcanninghistory.html.

49. "Coffee and Safety: Preventing Spills and Burns," *Coffee Enterprises*, February 9th, 2015, http://www.coffeeenterprises.com/2015/02/coffee-and-safety-preventing-spills-and-burns.

50. "Liebeck vs. McDonald's Restaurant," *Wikipedia,* https://en.wikipedia.org/wiki/Liebeck_v._McDonald%27s_Restaurants.

51. *Coffee Enterprises, Ibid.*

52. Carol Ann Rinzler, *The New Complete Book of Food*, (New York: Facts on File, 2009); "Coffee & Cholesterol," *NBC News*, http://www.nbc-

news.com/id/6242467/ns/health-heart_health/t/coffee-cholesterol/#. WBY3Xb00G5R.

53.    C. Cavin, D. Holzhaeuser, G. Sharf, A. Constable, W. W. Huber, and B. Schilter, "Cafestol and Kahweol, Two Coffee Specific Diterpenes with Anticarcinogenic Activity," *Food and Chemical Toxicology*, August 2002, 40(8):1155–63, https://www.ncbi.nlm.nih.gov/pubmed/12067578.

54.    Larry Hand, "Moderate Tea Drinking Tea May Slow CAC Progression, Cut CV Event Risk: MESA," *Medscape,* September 23, 2016, http://www.medscape.com/viewarticle/869038?nlid=109439_3901&src=wnl_newsalrt_160923_MSC-PEDIT&uac=77550DZ&impID=1202658&faf=1.

55.    H. Wang, Y. Wen, Y. Du, X. Yan, H. Guo, J.A Rycroft, N. Boon, E.M. Kovacs, D.J. Mela, "Effects of Catechin Enriched Green Tea on Body Composition," *Obesity,* April 18, 2010, (4):773–9, hpps://www.ncbi.nlm.nih.gov/pubmed/19680234.

56.    "FDA Consumer Advice on Pure Powdered Caffeine," *Food and Drug Administration,* updated December 7, 2015, http://www.fda.gov/Food/RecallsOutbreaksEmergencies/SafetyAlertsAdvisories/ucm405787.htm.

57.    "Caffeine Chart,"Center for Science in the Public Interest, https://cspinet.org/eating-healthy/ingredients-of-concern/caffeine-chart.

58.    "Energy Drinks," *National Center for Complementary and Integrative Health,* modified December 19, 2016, https://nccih.nih.gov/health/energy-drinks.

59.    *Ibid.*

60.    Nicole McEwen, "How to Avoid Getting Sick This Year," *Lifescript,* January 15, 2017, http://www.lifescript.com/health/centers/cold_flu/articles/germiest_public_places_top_8_to_avoid.aspx?utm_source=aol&utm_medium=syn&utm_campaign=Coldflu#sthash.vk0GzT6M.uMvFlE7J.dpuf.

61.    "Baby Weekender: Restaurant High Chairs," *Consumer Reports News*, June 26, 2009, http://www.consumerreports.org/cro/news/2009/06/baby-weekender-restaurant-high-chairs/index.htm.

62. David Pitt, "Experts: Health Risks Higher from Packaged Greens," *USA Today,* August 1, 2013, http://www.usatoday.com/story/news/nation/2013/08/01/health-risks-packaged-greens/2610153/.

63. Maggie Moon, "The 5 Worst Chain Restaurant Meals (and 5 Better Options)," *Livestrong,* Updated, September 7, 2016, http://www.livestrong.com/slideshow/1011240-5-worst-chain-restaurant-options-5-betterforyou-picks/?icid=maing-grid7%7Cmain5%7Cdl11%7Csec1_lnk3%26pLid%3D-685554593_htmlws-main-bb#slide=4.

64. Http://www.mcdonalds.com/us/en-us/about-our-food/nutrition-calculator.html#category.

65. Http://www.fatsecret.com/calories-nutrition/search?q=Wendy%27s+Salads.

66. Http://www.fatsecret.com/calories-nutrition/search?q=Burger+King+Salads.

67. Sarah Klein, "Food Safety at the Salad Bar," *Nutrition Action,* October 10, 014, http://www.nutritionaction.com/daily/food-safety/food-safety-at-the-salad-bar/.

68. "Plants Respond to Leaf Vibrations Caused by Insects' Chewing, MU Study Finds," *MU News,* July 01, 2014, http://munews.missouri.edu/news-releases/2014/0701-plants-respond-to-leaf-vibrations-caused-by-insects%E2%80%99-chewing-mu-study-finds/.

69. Nicholas Bakalar, "Eating Hot Peppers May Help You Live Longer," *The New York Times,* January 17, 2017, https://www.nytimes.com/2017/01/17/well/eat/eat-peppers-live-longer.html?_r=1.

70. Jun Lv, *et. al.,* "Consumption of spicy foods and total and cause specific mortality: population based cohort study," *British Medical Journal,* August 4, 2015, http://www.bmj.com/content/351/bmj.h3942.

71. Nicholas Bakalar, *Ibid.*

72. The scientific name for the condition of too much carotene in your blood is *carotenemia* or *xanthanemia.*

73. Ian D. Stephen, Vinet Coetzee, and David L. Perrett, "Carotenoid and Melanin Pigment Coloration Affect Perceived Human Health,"

*Evolution and Human Behavior,* May 2011, 32 (3) 216–227, http://
www.sciencedirect.com/science/article/pii/S1090513810001169.

74.  "Annals of Medicine," *The New Yorker,* May 27, 1967, http://www.
newyorker.com/magazine/1967/05/27/the-orange-man.

75.  Jan Hoffmandec, "Hallucinogen Eases Depression in Cancer Patients,
Studies Find," *The New York Times,* December 1, 2016, http://www.
nytimes.com/2016/12/01/health/hallucinogenic-mushrooms-psilocy-
bin-cancer-anxiety-depression.html.

76.  Suzanne Wu, "Meat and Cheese May Be as Bad as Smoking," *USC
News,* March 4, 2014, https://news.usc.edu/59199/meat-and-cheese-
may-be-as-bad-for-you-as-smoking/.

77.  The exception is *dietary fiber,* a polysaccharide whose sugar units are
bound so tightly together that the human gut cannot separate them—
which is why you can't digest hay.

78.  The % Daily Value is based on the 2015–2020 *Dietary Guidelines
for Americans* recommendation that no more than 10 percent of your
daily calories come from added sugars. "Changes to Nutrition Facts
Label," *US Food & Drug Administration,* http://www.fda.gov/Food/
GuidanceRegulation/GuidanceDocumentsRegulatoryInformation/
LabelingNutrition/ucm385663.htm.

79.  "Added Sugar in the Diet," *The Nutrition Source,* 2016, https://www.
hsph.harvard.edu/nutritionsource/carbohydrates/added-sugar-in-the-
diet/.

80.  "What is High-Fructose Corn Syrup? What are the Health Concerns?
Answers from Katherine Zeratsky, R.D., L.D.," *Mayo Clinic,* http://
www.mayoclinic.org/healthy-lifestyle/nutrition-and-healthy-eating/
expert-answers/high-fructose-corn-syrup/faq-20058201.

81.  Sarah Shireen Gul; A. Rebecca L. Hamilton, Alexander R. Munoz,
Tanit Phupitakphol, Wei Liu, Sanjiv K. Hyoju, Konstantinos P.
Economopoulos, Sara P. Morrison, Dong Hu Weifeng Zhang,
Mohammad Hadi Gharedaghi, Haizhong Huo, Sulaiman R. Ham-
arneh, and Richard A. Hodin, "Inhibition of the Gut Enzyme
Intestinal Alkaline Phosphatase May Explain How Aspartame

Promotes Glucose Intolerance and Obesity in Mice," *NRC Research Press*, November 18, 2016, http://www.nrcresearchpress.com/doi/abs/10.1139/apnm-2016-0346#.WExjWr00G5R.

82.  Christian Nordqvist, "How Safe Is Splenda? Is Splenda Bad For You?" *MNT*, updated May 29, 2015, http://www.medicalnewstoday.com/articles/262475.php.

83.  Julian Ryall and James Rothwell, "Ice Cream for Breakfast Makes You Smarter, Japanese Scientist Claims," *The Telegraph,* November 23, 2016, http://www.telegraph.co.uk/news/2016/11/23/ice-cream-breakfast-makes-smarter-japanese-scientist-claims/.

84.  Katarzyna Stolarz-Skrzypek, Tatiana Kuznetsova, Lutgarde Thijs, *et al*, "Fatal and Nonfatal Outcomes, Incidence of Hypertension, and Blood Pressure Changes in Relation to Urinary Sodium Excretion," *JAMANet*, May 4, 2011, http://jamanetwork.com/journals/jama/fullarticle/899663.

85.  *2015–2020 Dietary Guidelines for Americans,* https://health.gov/dietaryguidelines/2015/.

86.  Annie Britton, Archana Singh-Manoux, and Michael Marmot, "Alcohol Consumption and Cognitive Function in the Whitehall II Study*,"* *American Journal of Epidemiology*, August 1,2004, 160 (3), http://aje.oxfordjournals.org/content/160/3/240.long; I. Lang, R.B. Wallace, F.A. Huppert, and D. Melzer, "Moderate Alcohol Consumption in Older Adults is Associated with Better Cognition and Well-Being than Abstinence," *Age Ageing*, May 2007, 36(3):256–61, https://www.ncbi.nlm.nih.gov/pubmed/17353234.

87.  Carol Ann Rinzler, *Nutrition for Dummies*, 6th edition, (Hoboken, New Jersey: John Wiley & Sons, 2016).

88.  "What is a Standard Drink?" *National Institute of Alcohol Abuse and Alcoholism (NUAAA),* https://niaaa.nih.gov/alcohol-health/overview-alcohol-consumption/what-standard-drink.

89.  "The Dangers of Raw Milk: Unpasteurized Milk Can Pose a Serious Health Risk," *Food and Drug Administration*, updated September 3, 2015, http://www.fda.gov/Food/FoodborneIllnessContaminants/BuyStoreServeSafeFood/ucm079516.htm.

90.  "Mercury and Pregnancy," *The March of Dimes*, 2014, http://www. marchofdimes.org/pregnancy/mercury.aspx.

91.  Sascha Watkins, "What's Not Safe to Eat in Pregnancy," *Baby Centre*, http://www.babycentre.co.uk/x568574/whats-not-safe-to-eat-in-pregnancy#ixzz31nqykxxh.

92.  "Albacore," *Etymology Online,* http://www.etymonline.com/index. php?term=albacore.

93.  "Mercury in Canned Tuna Still a Concern," *Consumer Reports*, reviewed January 2011, http://www.consumerreports.org/cro/magazine-archive/2011/january/food/mercury-in-tuna/overview/index. htm.

94.  "Albacore," *Etymology Online*, http://www.etymonline.com/index. php?term=albacore= alba.

95.  "Tuna," *Wikipedia,* https://en.wikipedia.org/wiki/Tuna.

96.  Rutgers Researchers Debunk 'Five-Second Rule': Eating Food off the Floor Isn't Safe Sometimes bacteria can transfer in less than a second," *Rutgers University,* Thursday, September 8, 2016, http://news.rutgers. edu/research-news/rutgers-researchers-debunk-%E2%80%98five-second-rule%E2%80%99-eating-food-floor-isn%E2%80%99t-safe/20160908#.V-q35700G5R.

97.  Microbes that live naturally in your intestines but whose presence elsewhere suggests fecal contamination.

98.  Aaron E. Carroll, "I'm a Doctor. If I Drop Food on the Kitchen Floor, I Still Eat It," *The New York Times*, October 10, 2016, http:// www.nytimes.com/2016/10/11/upshot/im-a-doctor-if-i-drop-food-on-the-kitchen-floor-i-still-eat-it.html?_r=0.

99.  Carol Ann Rinzler, *Heartburn and Reflux for Dummies*, (New York: Wiley Publishing Inc., 2004).

100.  Jamie Koufman, "The Dangers of Eating Late At Night," *The New York Times*, October 25, 2014, http://www.nytimes.com/2014/10/26/ opinion/sunday/the-dangers-of-eating-late-at-night.html?_r=0.

101.  "Ten Beach Dangers Everyone Should Watch Out For," *AOL*, updated April 5, 2014, http://www.aol.com/chstrip.jsp.

102. "Death by Coconut," *Wikipedia*, https://en.wikipedia.org/wiki/Death_by_coconut.

103. Maryadele J. O'Neil, *The Merck Index*, 13th edition (Whitehoue Station, N.J.: Merck & Co., Inc, 2001).

104. Timo E. Strandberg. Sture Andersson, Anna-Liisa Järvenpää, and Paul M. McKeigue, "Preterm Birth and Licorice Consumption during Pregnancy," *American Journal of Epidemiology*, 2002, 156 (9): 803–805, https://academic.oup.com/aje/article/156/9/803/256317/Preterm-Birth-and-Licorice-Consumption-during.

105. Cavities in the bones in your head continuous with the inside of your nostrils.

# 3
# Health

106. Anahad O'Connor, "The Claim: Never Blow Your Nose When You Have a Cold," *The New York Times*, February 9, 2009, http://www.nytimes.com/2009/02/10/health/10real.html.

107. "What's Causing My Cold?" *WebMD*, January 20, 2015, http://www.webmd.com/cold-and-flu/cold-guide/common_cold_causes.

108. "Scientists Develop New Flu Vaccines for Man's Best Friend," *Phys. org*, January 26, 2017, https://phys.org/news/2017-01-scientists-flu-vaccines-friend.html#jCp.

109. J.J.M. Askanasy, "The Photic Sneeze," *Postgrad Medical Journal*, 1990, 66, 892–893, https://www.ncbi.nlm.nih.gov/pmc/articles/PMC2429753/pdf/postmedj00167-0007; C. Sevillano, A. Parafita-Fernández, V. Rodriguez-Lopez, M. Sampil, N. Moraña, E. Viso, and F.J. Cores, "A Curious Fact: Photic Sneeze Reflex. Autosomical Dominant Compelling Helio-Ophthalmic Outburst Syndrome," *Archivos de la Sociedad Espanola de Oftalmologia* [in English], July 2016, 91(7):305–9, https://www.ncbi.nlm.nih.gov/pubmed/26896062.

110.     "Kissing and Your health," *Department of Health & Human Services, State Government of Victoria, Australia,* 2016, https://www.better-health.vic.gov.au/health/conditionsandtreatments/kissing-and-your-health.

111.     "A French kiss is so-called because at the beginning of the twenti-eth century, in the English-speaking world, the French had acquired a reputation for more adventurous and passionate sex practices. In France, it is referred to as *un baiser amoureux* ("a lover's kiss") or *un baiser avec la langue* ("a kiss with the tongue"), even if in past times it was also known as *baiser Florentin* ("Florentine kiss"). The *Petit Robert 2014 French* dictionary, released on May 30, 2013, add-ed the French verb "se galocher"—slang for kissing with tongues—making it the first time a single word described the practice (except in Quebec, where the verb "frencher" means French kissing; Aus-tralia, where the term "pash" is used; the German verb "knutschen"; the Italian verb "limonare'; and the Hungarian verb 'megcsókol/csókolózik')";"French kiss," *Wikipedia,* https://en.wikipedia.org/wiki/French_kiss.

112.     Email correspondence, January 13, 2017; Mark Sklansky, Nikhil Nadkami, and Lynn Ramirez-Avila, "Banning the Handshake from the Health Care Setting," *The Jama Network*, June 25, 2014, http://jamanetwork.com/journals/jama/fullarticle/1873637.

113.     Paula Mason, "Nothing Smaller Than your Elbow, Please," *American Speech Language Hearing Association*, 2015, http://www.asha.org/uploadedFiles/AIS-Earwax.pdf.

114.     "In a 1997 article in the *British Medical Journal*, Michael Peel, senior medical examiner at the Medical Foundation for the Care of Victims of Torture, cites well-documented studies reporting survivals of oth-er hunger strikers for twenty-eight, thirty-six, thirty-eight, and for-ty days. [Editor's Note: Reports of the 1981 hunger strike by politi-cal prisoners against the British presence in Northeast Ireland indicate that ten individuals died after periods of between forty-six and sev-enty-three days without food.]; Alan D. Lieberson, "How long can a

person survive without food?" *Scientific American*, 2016, https://www. scientificamerican.com/article/how-long-can-a-person-sur/.

115.   Marion Wallace Dunlop, *Wikipedia*, https://en.wikipedia.org/wiki/ Marion_Wallace_Dunlop; *Scientific American, Ibid.*

116.   "Cesar's Last Fast," http://cesarslastfast.com/?page_id=7.

117.   "Students' Hunger Strike at the 1989 Tiananmen Square Protests," *Wikipedia*, https://en.wikipedia.org/wiki/Students%27_hunger_ strike_at_the_1989_Tiananmen_Square_protests.

118.   "Richard Branson to Take Over as Mia Farrow Ends Hunger Strike," *The Telegraph*, May 9, 2009, http://www.telegraph.co.uk/news/celeb- ritynews/5298439/Richard-Branson-to-take-over-as-Mia-Farrow- ends-hunger-strike.html.

119.   Shanna Freeman, "How Water Works," *How Stuff Works,* http://sci- ence.howstuffworks.com/environmental/earth/geophysics/h2o3.htm.

120.   Protein in your muscles, hair and fingernails accounts for about 16 percent of your body mass; minerals such as calcium for about 6 percent; carbs for about 1 percent. "Chemical Composition of the Human Body," *About Education,* http://chemistry.about.com/ od/chemicalcomposition/a/Chemical-Composition-Of-The-Hu- man-Body.htm.

121.   Freeman, *Ibid.*

122.   Aaron E. Carroll, "No, You Do Not Have to Drink 8 Glasses of Water a Day," *The New York Times*, August 25, 2015, http://www. nytimes.com/2015/08/25/upshot/no-you-do-not-have-to-drink-8- glasses-of-water-a-day.html?_r=0.

123.   Carol Ann Rinzler, *Nutrition for Dummies, Ibid.*

124.   "Selecting and Effectively Using Hydration for Fitness," *American College of Sports Medicine, n.d.,* http://www.acsm.org/docs/brochures/ selecting-and-effectively-using-hydration-for-fitness.pdf.

125.   Laura Christine Lee and Maryann Noronha, "When Plenty is Too Much: Water Intoxication in a Patient with a Simple Urinary Tract Infection,"*BMJ Case Reports 2016*, November 1, 2016, http://casere- ports.bmj.com/content/2016/bcr-2016-216882.

# Endnotes

126.    "Study Debunks Common Myth That Urine is Sterile," *Loyola University Health System,* May 18, 2014, http://www.newswise.com/articles/view/617820/?sc=mwtr&xy=5003042.

127.    Does the title *Go Ask Alice* seem familiar? If so, you may be revealing your age by remembering the similarly titled 1971 "autobiography" of an unhappy fictional teenager: "Go Ask Alice," *Wikipedia,* https://en.wikipedia.org/wiki/Go_Ask_Alice; "Consequences of Holding Your Pee," *GoAskAlice!,* updated June 2, 2015, http://goaskalice.columbia.edu/answered-questions/consequences-holding-your-pee

128.    http://www.waterandhealth.org/

129.    Jalecsa Baulkman, "Peeing In Swimming Pools May Cause Heart, Lung Problems," *University Herald*, March 26, 2014, http://www.universityherald.com/articles/8404/20140326/peeing-in-swimming-pools-may-cause-lung-heart-problems.htm; Ann Miller, "The Truth About What Happens in the Pool," *The Daily Dose*, August 22, 2015, http://www.ozy.com/acumen/the-truth-about-what-happens-in-the-pool/33079?utm_source–AOL1&utm_medium=cpc&utm_campaign=cpc%E2%80%8B&icid=maing-grid7%7Cmain5%7C-dl40%7Csec1_lnk3%26pLid%3D1263705741_htmlws-main-bb.

130.    Clara Curtin, "Fact or Fiction?: Urinating on a Jellyfish Sting is an Effective Treatment," *Scientific American*, January4, 2007, https://www.scientificamerican.com/article/fact-or-fiction-urinating/; "Osmosis," Merriam-Webster, https://www.merriam-webster.com/dictionary/osmosis.

131.    "Australia, though, has nastier jellyfish (such as the deadly Box Jellyfish) and most Australian lifeguard teams are equipped with morphine and antivenoms to treat unlucky swimmers Down Under." Curtin, *Ibid.*

132.    Sarah C. Markt, Elizabeth Nuttall, Constance Turman, Jennifer Sinnott, Eric B. Rimm, Ethan Ecsedy, Robert H. Unger, Katja Fall, Stephen Finn, Majken K. Jensen, Jennifer R. Rider, Peter Kraft, and Lorelei A. Mucci, "Sniffing Out Significant 'Pee Values': Genome Wide Association Study of Asparagus Anosmia," *British Medical*

*Journal,* December 13, 2016, http://www.bmj.com/content/355/bmj. i6071.

133. Joseph Stromberg, "Why Asparagus Makes Your Urine Smell," *Smithsonian,* May 3, 2013, http://www.smithsonianmag.com/science-nature/why-asparagus-makes-your-urine-smell-49961252/#ELJ6JF4ps-Dy2mmSG.99.

134. "Nonfatal Bathroom Injuries Among Persons Aged ≥ 15 Years— United States, 2008," *CDC Morbidity and Mortality Weekly Report (MMWR),* June 10, 2011, 60(22), 729–733, https://www.cdc.gov/mmwr/preview/mmwrhtml/mm6022a1.htm.

135. Rachel Nussbaum, "When's the Best Time to Shower: Morning or Night?" *Greatist,* August 20, 2015, http://greatist.com/grow/best-time-to-shower.

136. "Can I Get Struck by Lightning When I'm Indoors?" *How Stuff Works, n.d.,* http://science.howstuffworks.com/nature/climate-weather/storms/question681.htm.

137. "Nonfatal Bathroom Injuries Among Persons Aged >15 Years," *CDC, Ibid.*

138. "The Use and Handling of Toothbrushes," *Centers for Disease Control and Prevention,* Updated July 10, 2013, http://www.cdc.gov/oralhealth/infectioncontrol/factsheets/toothbrushes.htm; "Clean Before You Clean—What's On Your Toothbrush Just Might Surprise You,*"* *Science Daily,* May 6, 2014, https://www.sciencedaily.com/releases/2014/05/140506094439.htm2014.

139. "Addis," *Wikipedia,* https://en.wikipedia.org/wiki/William_Addis_ (entrepreneur); Elizabeth Nix, "Who Invented the Toothbrush?" *Ask History,* August 22, 2012, http://www.history.com/news/ask-history/who-invented-the-toothbrush; "Who Invented the Toothbrush," *Science Illustrated,* April 26, 2012, http://scienceillustrated.com.au/blog/ask-us/who-invented-the-toothbrush/.

140. "Toothpaste Allergy," *allergysynmptomsx,* n.d., http://allergysymptomsx.com/toothpaste-allergy.php.

141.    Catherine Saint Louis, "Why a Chemical Banned from Soap Is Still in Your Toothpaste," *The New York Times,* September 7, 2016, http://www.nytimes.com/2016/09/07/well/live/why-your-toothpaste-has-triclosan.html?utm_campaign=KHN:+First+Edition&utm_source=hs_email&utm_medium=email&utm_content=33922464&_hsenc=p2ANqtz--.

142.    Catherine Saint Louis, "Feeling Guilty About Not Flossing? Maybe There's No Need," *The New York Times,* August 2, 2016, https://www.nytimes.com/2016/08/03/health/flossing-teeth-cavities.html?_r=0.

143.    "Is It More Effective to Floss Teeth with a Water Pick or Standard Dental Floss?," *Mayo Clinic,* February 18, 2015, http://www.mayoclinic.org/healthy-lifestyle/adult-health/expert-answers/dental-floss/faq-20058112.

144.    Catherine Saint Louis, "Feeling Guilty About Not Flossing? Maybe There's No Need," *The New York Times,* August 2, 2016, http://www.nytimes.com/2016/08/03/health/flossing-teeth-cavities.html?_r=0; Annie Behr, "String of Lies," *Slate,* August 4, 2016, http://www.slate.com/articles/health_and_science/medical_examiner/2016/08/the_data_for_or_against_floss_is_biased_and_terrible.html.

145.    "Toothpick," *Wikipedia,* https://en.wikipedia.org/wiki/Toothpick.

146.    "Toothpicks: For Hors d'Oeuvres, Not teeth," *Mayo Clinic,* n.d., http://www.mayoclinic.org/healthy-lifestyle/adult-health/in-depth/health-tip/art-20048779.

147.    *Guinness World Records,* http://www.guinnessworldrecords.com/news/2012/10/video-irishman-sets-new-record-set-for-the-most-toothpicks-in-a-beard-45278/.

148.    Susan Scutti, "Is Your Hand Sanitizer Safe? The FDA Wants to Know," *CNN,* updated June 30, 2016, http://www.cnn.com/2016/06/30/health/fda-hand-sanitizers/index.html.

149.    Roni Caryn Rabin, "Don't Drink the Hand Sanitizer," *The New York Times,* October 24, 2016, http://www.nytimes.com/2016/10/24/well/live/dont-drink-the-hand-sanitizer.html?_r=0.

150.   "When & How to Wash Your Hands," *Centers for Disease Control and Prevention,* September 4, 2015, http://www.cdc.gov/handwashing/when-how-handwashing.html.

151.   David Elliot, "The Glenn A. Fry Award Lecture 2013: Blurred Vision, Spectacle Correction, and Falls in Older Adults," *Optometry & Vision Science,* June 2014, 91 (6), 593–601, http://journals.lww.com/optvissci/Abstract/2014/06000/The_Glenn_A__Fry_Award_Lecture_2013___Blurred.3.aspx.

152.   C. Clayborne Ray, "A Scientific Lens on Copper," *The New York Times*, January 23, 2017, https://www.nytimes.com/2017/01/23/science/copper-bracelets-arthritis.html.

153.   "New Theory as to Why Some People Die during Sleep," *Medical Net*, August 9, 2005, http://www.news-medical.net/news/2005/08/09/12336.aspx.

154.   "Obstructive Sleep Apnea Severity Linked with Death Risk," *Huffington Post*, updated Feb 29, 2016, http://www.huffingtonpost.com/2013/10/21/obstructive-sleep-apnea-death-risk-mortality_n_4124716.html.

155.   "Now I Lay Me Down to Sleep," *Wikipedia,* https://en.wikipedia.org/wiki/Now_I_Lay_Me_Down_to_Sleep.

156.   Edwin McDowell, "'A Light in the Attic' Sets Best Seller Record," *The New York Times,* January 10, 1985, http://www.nytimes.com/1985/01/10/books/a-light-in-the-attic-sets-best-seller-record.html.

157.   Bart Jansen, "Driving on 5 Hours Sleep Is Like Driving Drunk," *USA Today*, December 6, 2016, http://www.usatoday.com/story/news/2016/12/06/driving-5-hours-sleep-like-driving-drunk/94992718/Driving on 5 hours of sleep is like driving drunk.

158.   Peter Russell, "Better Sleep 'Boosts Sex Life for Older Women,'" WebMD UK, February 1, 2017, http://www.webmd.boots.com/sleep-disorders/news/20170201/better-sleep-boosts-sex-life.

159.   First figures indicate low end "acceptable," second, high end. "National Sleep Foundation Recommends New Sleep Times," *National Sleep*

*Foundation*, 2016, https://sleepfoundation.org/media-center/press-re-lease/national-sleep-foundation-recommends-new-sleep-times.

160.  First figures suggest sleep deprivation; second may suggest an under-lying problem requiring more sleep than normal. "National Sleep Foundation Recommends New Sleep Times," *National Sleep Founda-tion*, 2016, https://sleepfoundation.org/media-center/press-release/national-sleep-foundation-recommends-new-sleep-times.

# 4

# Sports & Other Athletic Endeavors

161.  Sonya Collins, "The Truth About Stretching," *WebMD,* 2012, http://www.webmd.com/fitness-exercise/guide/how-to-stretch#1.

162.  *Ibid.*

163.  "Keeping Your Balance as You Age," *Berkeley Wellness,* November 1, 2011, http://www.berkeleywellness.com/fitness/injury-prevention/article/keeping-your-balance-you-age.

164.  "League of Denial, the NFL's Concussion Crisis," *Frontline*, October 9, 2013, http://www.pbs.org/wgbh/frontline/film/league-of-denial/.

165.  "NFL Injury Reports," *Frontline*, updated January 25, 2015, http://apps.frontline.org/concussion-watch/#positions_2015.

166.  Joseph A. Rosenthal, Randi E. Foraker, Christy L. Collins, and R. Dawn Comstock, "National High School Athlete Concus-sion Rates From 2005–2006 to 2011–2012," *American Journal of Sports Medicine*, April 16, 2014, http://journals.sagepub.com/doi/abs/10.1177/0363546514530091.

167.  "NFL Injury Reports," *Frontline*, updated January 25, 2015, http://apps.frontline.org/concussion-watch/#positions_2015.

168. "Sport Concussion Statistics," *Headcase Company.com*, 2013, http://www.headcasecompany.com/concussion_info/stats_on_concussions_sports.

169. "Muscles used in kicking," Reference.com, 2016, https://www.reference.com/science/muscles-used-kicking-38017943abc9aa4d.

170. A.T. Tysyaer, "Head and Neck Injuries in Soccer. Impact of Minor Trauma," *Sports Medicine*, September 1992, https://www.ncbi.nlm.nih.gov/pubmed/1439395?dopt=Abstract.

171. Eric H. Chudler, "Neuroscience for Kids: Soccer and the Brain," *University of Washington*, updated December 16, 2016, http://faculty.washington.edu/chudler/soccer.html.

172. "Hazard Screening Report, Sports Activities and Equipment (Excluding Major Team Sports)," *US Consumer Product Safety Commission*, 2005, http://www.cpsc.gov/PageFiles/106120/hazard_sports.pdf.

173. Brock Ray, "How Dangerous is Hunting, Really?" *InterstateSportsman*, 2017, http://www.interstatesportsman.com/articles/how-dangerous-is-hunting-really.

174. "Injury Facts® 2016 Edition," *National Safety Council*, http://www.nsc.org/learn/safety-knowledge/Pages/injury-facts-chart.aspx.

175. David Hemenway, "Risks and Benefits of a Gun in the Home," *American Journal of Lifestyle Medicine*, February 2, 2011, http://journals.sagepub.com/doi/abs/10.1177/1559827610396294.

176. "ACP Applauds Federal Appeals Court Decision Overturning Unconstitutional Florida Ban on Physicians Counseling Patients on Gun Safety," *American College of Physicians*, February 17, 2017, https://www.acponline.org/acp-newsroom/acp-applauds-federal-appeals-court-decision-overturning-unconstitutional-florida-ban-on-physicians.

177. Matthew J. Thompson and Frederick P. Rivara, "Bicycle related injuries," *American Family Physician*, May 15, 2001, http://www.aafp.org/afp/2001/0515/p2007.html.

178. Mona Chalabi, "Is skiing the world's most dangerous sport?" *The Guardian*, December 30, 2013, https://www.theguardian.com/news/

# Endnotes

datablog/2013/dec/30/is-skiing-the-worlds-most-dangerous-sport; "Avalanches," *National Geographic*, 2016–1017, http://environment.nationalgeographic.com/environment/natural-disasters/avalanche-profile/; Colorado Avalanche Information Center, http://avalanche.state.co.us/accidents/us/.

179.    "Medication Guide," *Allergen*, revised January, 2016, http://www.allergan.com/miscellaneous-pages/allergan-pdf-files/botox_med_guide.

180.    "Duke EWG Study finds Toxic Nail Polish Chemicals in Women's Bodies," *EWG*, October 19, 2015, http://www.ewg.org/release/duke-ewg-study-finds-toxic-nail-polish-chemical-women-s-bodies; Deborah Blum, "Ask Well: Is Nail Polish Harmful?," *The New York Times*, January 2, 2014, http://well.blogs.nytimes.com/2014/01/02/ask-well-is-nail-polish-harmful/?_r=0.

181.    "Stay Healthy and Safe While Giving Manicures and Pedicures," *OSHA*, 2012, https://www.osha.gov/Publications/3542nail-salon-workers-guide.pdf.

182.    Daniel DeNoon, "UV Nail Lamps Safe, Study Suggests," *WebMD,* December, 6, 2012, http://www.webmd.com/cancer/news/20121205/uv-nail-lamps-safe#1.

183.    Liesa Goins, "Are Gel Manicures Safe?" *WebMD*, reviewed September 23, 2014, http://www.webmd.com/beauty/features/gel-manicure-safety#2.

184.    Lawrence E. Gibson, "Can I Harm My Natural Nails by Wearing Acrylic Nails?" *Mayo Clinic,* February 4, 2015, http://www.mayoclinic.org/healthy-lifestyle/adult-health/expert-answers/acrylic-nails/faq-20057849.

185.    "Longest Fingernails on a Pair of Hands (Female)—Ever," *Guinness World Records*, http://www.guinnessworldrecords.com/world-records/longest-fingernails-(female)-ever.

186.    "Shridhaur Chillal," *Wikipedia*, December 16, 2016, https://en.wikipedia.org/wiki/Shridhar_Chillal.

187.    "Nail Biting: Topic Overview," *WebMD*, http://www.webmd.com/anxiety-panic/tc/nail-biting-topic-overview#1.

188.    Jessika Toothman and Ann Meeker, "How Hair Dryers Work," *Howstuffworks,* http://home.howstuffworks.com/hair-dryer4.htm; "Ground Faulty Circuit Interrupters Can Save a Life," *ConnairCanada,* n.d., http://www.conaircanada.ca/pdf/en/ibs/en_DS-224R.pdf; "Electrified Bathtub," *TV Tropes,* http://tvtropes.org/pmwiki/pmwiki.php/Main/ElectrifiedBathtub.

189.    Rebecca Guenard, "Hair Dye: A History," *The Atlantic,* January 2, 2015, http://www.theatlantic.com/health/archive/2015/01/hair-dye-a-history/383934; "When in doubt, the European Commission bans the use of a particular chemical. In 2006, then-European Commission Vice-President Günter Verheugen said in a press release: 'Substances for which there is no proof that they are safe will disappear from the market. Our high safety standards do not only protect E.U. consumers, they also give legal certainty to European cosmetics industry.' It has prohibited 22 hair-dye chemicals so far—and more are likely to be added to the list, which is updated annually. Most recently, the SCCP deemed 2-chloro-p-phenylenediamine, used to color eyebrows and lashes, unsafe on the grounds of insufficient toxicology data." Sarah Marshall, "When, and Why, Did Women Start Dyeing Their Gray Hair?" *Elle,* September 18, 2015, http://www.elle.com/beauty/hair/news/a30556/when-and-why-did-women-start-dyeing-their-gray-hair/.

190.    Diane Wedner, "Is Coloring Hair Safe? What Research Says About Hair Dyes and Cancer," *Lifescript,* March 7, 2014, http://www.lifescript.com/health/centers/cancer/articles/is_your_hair_dye_safe.aspx?utm_source=aol&utm_medium=syn&utm_campaign=cancer&icid=maing-grid7%7Cmain5%7Cdl15%7Csec3_lnk3%26pLid%3D1365322058_htmlws-main-bb#sthash.FyD-0CzBY.dpuf.

191.    Guenard, *Ibid.*

192.    "Hair Dye," *How Products Are Made,* http://www.madehow.com/Volume-3/Hair-Dye.html#ixzz4TtWOj8Sg.

193.    Guenard, *Ibid;* "Hair Coloring/Dying Statistics," *Statistic Brain,* March 14, 2015, http://www.statisticbrain.com/hair-coloring-dying-statistics/.

194.    Neil Katz, "Sweat Lodge Death Investigation Turns to Self-Help Guru James Arthur Ray," *CBS NEWS*, October 12, 2009, http://www.cbsnews.com/news/sweat-lodge-death-investigation-turns-to-self-help-guru-james-arthur-ray/.

195.    Angela Joseph, "The Dangers of Wrapping Your Stomach With Plastic Wrap," *Livestrong*, updated January 30, 2017, http://www.livestrong.com/article/373330-how-to-lose-weight-with-a-stomach-wrap/.

196.    "Tongue Piercing," *Wikipedia*, https://en.wikipedia.org/wiki/Tongue_piercing.

197.    "Star Trek Classic Spock Ears," https://www.amazon.com/Star-Trek-Classic-Spock-Ears/dp/B0029F1WOC/ref=sr_1_1?ie=UTF8&qid=1482338664&sr=8–1&keywords=dr+spock+ears.

198.    "Oral Piercings: What You Should Know," *WebMD,* reviewed May 24, 2016, http://www.webmd.com/oral-health/guide/oral-piercing#1.

199.    "Oral Piercing, Key Points," *ADA*, updated January 11, 2017, http://www.ada.org/en/member-center/oral-health-topics/oral-piercing.

200.    "Clinic Refuses Requests for 'Snake Eyes' Body Piercing," *Fox News,* October 20, 2016, http://www.foxnews.com/health/2016/10/20/clinic-refuses-requests-for-snake-eyes-body-piercing.html.

201.    "Oral Piercing, Key Points," *Ibid.*

202.    "Tongue Splitting," *Wikipedia*, https://en.wikipedia.org/wiki/Tongue_splitting.

203.    "Body Piercing Problems," *WebMD*, n.d., http://www.webmd.com/skin-problems-and-treatments/tc/body-piercing-problems-topic-overview#1; "Transdermal Implant," *Wikipedia*, https://en.wikipedia.org/wiki/Transdermal_implant.

204.    James Weber, "Surface Anchors, Punches, and Legislation Issues," *BME*, December 16, 2009, https://news.bme.com/2009/12/16/dermal-punches-and-surface-anchors/.

205.    "Think Before You Ink," *FDA*, Updated November 29, 2016, http://www.fda.gov/ForConsumers/ConsumerUpdates/ucm048919.htm.

206. Amanda L. Chan, "Nearly One-Third of People with Tattoos Regret Getting One: Study," *Huffington Post*, July 12, 2012, http://www.huffingtonpost.com/2012/07/12/tattoo-regret_n_1654959.html.

207. "Talcum Powder," *Drugwatch*, 2016, https://www.drugwatch.com/talcum-powder/.

208. *Ibid.*

209. Malcolm H. Moss, "Dangers from Talcum Powder," *Pediatrics,* June 1969, 43 (6), http://pediatrics.aappublications.org/content/43/6/1058.

210. Jeannette Moninger, "Choosing an Antiperspirant for Sensitive Skin," *WebMD*, n.d., http://www.webmd.com/skin-problems-and-treatments/features/antiperspirant-sensitive-skin#1; Grace Gold, "The Deodorant Ingredient Glossary," *Everyday Health*, updated January 21, 2o14, http://www.everydayhealth.com/news/the-deodorant-ingredient-glossary/ast.

211. "Tetrachloroethylene," *Wikipedia*, https://en.wikipedia.org/wiki/Tetrachloroethylene.

212. "USEPA Requirements for PERC Dry Cleaners," *NYS Environmental Facilities Corporation*, September 2013, http://www.nyc.gov/html/dep/pdf/perc_drycleaners.pdf.

213. Paul Pestano, "Cleaning Chemicals Hang Around—On Your Clothes," *EWG*, September 12, 2011, http://www.ewg.org/enviroblog/2011/09/dry-cleaning-chemicals-hang-around-your-clothes.

214. Gretchen Reynolds, "A Scientific Look at the Dangers of High Heels," *The New York Times*, January 25, 2012 , https://well.blogs.nytimes.com/2012/01/25/scientists-look-at-the-dangers-of-high-heels/.

215. Carol Ann Rinnzler, *Leonardo's Foot*, (New York: Bellevue Literary Press, 2013).

216. "AU Study Shows That Overuse of Flip-Flops Can Lead to Orthopedic Problems," *Wireeagle*, June 3, 2008, http://wireeagle.auburn.edu/news/359.

217.     S.M. Kramer, "Fact or Fiction? Underwire Bras Cause Cancer," *Scientific American.com*, April 19, 2007, https://www.scientificamerican.com/article/fact-or-fiction-underwire-bras-cause-cancer/.

# 6

# Music & Art & TV & Books & Travel & Weather & Paper & Pencils & Everything Else

218.     Hoai-Tran Bui, "Study: Watching Too Much TV Could Lead to Early Death," *USA Today*, June 25, 2014, http://www.usatoday.com/story/news/nation/2014/06/25/tv-television-early-death-premature-risk-sedentary/11366047/; Francisco Javier Basterra-Gortari, Maris Bes-Rastrollo, Alfredo Gea, Jorge María Núñez-Córdoba, Estefanía Toledo, and Miguel Angel Martínez-González, "Television Viewing, Computer Use, Time Driving and All-Cause Mortality: The SUN Cohort," *Journal of the American Heart Association*, June 25, 2014, http://jaha.ahajournals.org/content/3/3/e000864.

219.     "Headphone and Ear Bud Use Safety Guide*," Cleveland Clinic*, n.d., https://health.clevelandclinic.org/2014/02/headphone-and-ear-bud-use-safety-guide/.

220.     *Ibid.*

221.     "Warning to Teens. Loud Noise Now Can Cause Hearing Loss Later," *Pediatrics*, December 27, 2010, https://www.aap.org/en-us/about-the-aap/aap-press-room/Pages/Warning-to-Teens-Loud-Noise-Now-Can-Cause-Hearing-Loss-Later.aspx; Elizabeth Henderson, Marcia Testa, and Christopher Hartnick, "Prevalence of Noise-Induced Hearing-Threshold Shifts and Hearing Loss Among US Youths," *Pediat-*

*rics,* January 2011, 127 (1), http://pediatrics.aappublications.org/content/127/1/e39?maxtoshow=&RESULTFORMAT=&issue=1.

222.    Catherine Saint Louis, "Children's Headphones May Carry Risk of Hearing Loss," *The New York Times,* December 6, 2016, http://www.nytimes.com/2016/12/06/health/headphones-hearing-loss-kids.html?hp&action=click&pgtype=Homepage&clickSource=story-heading&module=second-column-region&region=top-news&WT.nav=top-news&_r=0.

223.    Steve Claridge, "How Loud Is Too Loud: Decibel Levels of Common Sounds," *Hearingaidknow,* 2006, https://www.hearingaidknow.com/how-loud-is-too-loud-decibel-levels-of-common-sounds.

224.    The Reverend Danger, "The Top 10 Deaths Caused by Video Games, *Spike.com*, February 24, 2009, http://www.spike.com/articles/id98jf/the-top-10-deaths-caused-by-video-games.

225.    Daisy Fancourt, Thomas M.W. Burton, and Aaron Williamon, "The Razor's Edge: Australian Rock Music Impairs Men's Performance When Pretending to Be a Surgeon," *Medical Journal of Australia,* 2016; 205 (11): 515–518, https://www.mja.com.au/journal/2016/205/11/razor-s-edge-australian-rock-music-impairs-men-s-performance-when-pretending-be.

226.    "Category: Executed Writers," *Wikipedia*, https://en.wikipedia.org/wiki/Category:Executed_writers.

227.    Raleigh began writing but never completed a manuscript titled *The Historie of the World* while imprisoned in the Tower of London.

228.    "Jacques Fesch," *Mother of God,* n.d., http://motheofgod.com/threads/jacques-fesch.6138/.

229.    "Banned and Challenged Books," *Goodreads,* https://www.goodreads.com/list/tag/banned.

230.    Sara J. Brook, "Are Public Library Books Contaminated by Bacteria?," *Journal of Clinical Epidemiology,* October 1994, 47 (10), http://www.sciencedirect.com/science/article/pii/0895435694901031.

## Endnotes

231.   Emma Penrod, "Research Team Seeks Answers on How Dirty the Library Is," *The Daily Universe*, December 4, 2011, http://universe. byu.edu/2011/12/04/dirty-library-books.

232.   Leonard Greene, "Library Books Turn Out to be 'Fifty Shades' of Gross," *New York Post*, November 14, 2013, http://nypost. com/2013/11/14/library-books-turn-out-to-be-fifty-shades-of-gross/.

233.   "This is the Safest Place to Sit on a Plane," *Time* Magazine, June 25, 2015, http://time.com/3934663/safest-seat-airplane/.

234.   Claire Maldarelli, "How to prevent blood clots as airlines squeeze you into tighter spaces," *AOL*, May 8, 2017, https://www.aol.com/article/news/2017/05/08/how-to-prevent-blood-clots-as-airlines-squeeze-you-into-tighter/22075464/.

235.   Pete Donohue, "Deaths by New York Subway Train Strikes Shrank Slightly for 2013, MTA says," *New York Daily News*, December 31, 2013, http://www.nydailynews.com/new-york/nyc-subway-train-deaths-decrease-2013-mta-article-1.1562928.

236.   Hamid Aleaziz, "BART launches campaign after recent suicides on the tracks," *SF Gate,* updated April 14, 2015, http://www.sfgate. com/bayarea/article/BART-launches-campaign-after-recent-suicides-on-6199858.php.

237.   Leighton Walter Kille, "Transportation Safety Over Time: Cars, Planes, Trains, Walking, Cycling," *Journalist's Resource*, updated October 5, 2014, https://journalistsresource.org/studies/environment/transportation/comparing-fatality-risks-united-states-transportation-across-modes-time#.

238.   Tanya Lewis, "Where Is the Safest Place to Sit on a Train?," *Live Science*, May 13, 2015, http://www.livescience.com/50827-safest-part-of-train.html.

239.   Elizabeth Howell, "Weightlessness and Its Effect on Astronauts," *Space.com*, September 30, 2013, http://www.space. com/23017-weightlessness.html.

240.   Claire Maldarelli, "NASA's Twin Study Reveals Space Travel Changes Human DNA," *AOL*, February 1, 2017, https://www.aol.com/arti-

cle/news/2017/02/01/nasa-twin-study-scott-mark-kelly-space-travel-changes-dna/21704465/.

241. "Telomeres and Cancer Mortality: The Long and the Short of It," *ScienceDaily*, April 10, 2015, https://www.sciencedaily.com/releases/2015/04/150410165312.htm.

242. Kate Gibson, "In Car Crashes, Backseat Can Be More Dangerous than the Front." *Moneywatch*, February 13, 2015, http://www.cbsnews.com/news/sitting-in-the-back-no-longer-the-safest-bet-for-all/.

243. Lois Baker, "A Car's Middle Back Seat May Be Least Desirable, but It's the Safest," *News Center University at Buffalo*, June 27, 2006, http://www.buffalo.edu/news/releases/2006/06/8026.html.

244. "Maine Revised Statutes," *Maine Legislature*, http://www.mainelegislature.org/legis/statutes/29-A/title29-Asec2057.html.

245. "Injury Facts® 2016 Edition," *National Safety Council*, http://www.nsc.org/learn/safety-knowledge/Pages/injury-facts-chart.aspx.

246. Pete Bigelow, "Pedestrian Deaths Increase; Cell-Phone Distractions May Be Culprit," *Autoblog*, August 13, 2015, http://www.autoblog.com/2015/08/13/pedestrian-deaths-increase-cell-phone-distractions/.

247. Erin Dooley, "Distracted Walking: How 'Petextrians' Are Endangering Our Streets," *ABC News*, August 10, 2015, http://abcnews.go.com/US/distracted-walking-petextrians-endangering-streets/story?id=32990067; "Injury Facts® 2016 Edition," *National Safety Council*, http://www.nsc.org/learn/safety-knowledge/Pages/injury-facts-chart.aspx.

248. Bigelow, *Ibid.*

249. "How Much Physical Activity Do Adults Need?" *Centers for Disease Control and Prevention,* reviewed June 4, 2015, https://www.cdc.gov/physicalactivity/basics/adults/index.htm.

250. "Stair Safety," *Nationwide Children's Hospital*, 2012, http://www.nationwidechildrens.org/cirp-stair-safety.

251. "12 Steps to Stair Safety at Home," *Public Health Agency of Canada*, modified December 13, 2013, http://www.phac-aspc.gc.ca/seniors-

aines/publications/public/injury-blessure/steps-escalier/index-eng.
php.

252. McEwen, Nicole, *Ibid.*

253. *Ibid.*

254. "NWS Weather Fatality, Injury and Damage Statistics," *National Oceanic and Atmospheric Administration (NOAA)*, updated April 6, 2016, http://www.nws.noaa.gov/om/hazstats/light14.pdf.

255. "Indoor Lightning Safety," *National Oceanic and Atmospheric Administration (NOAA)*, n.d., http://www.lightningsafety.noaa.gov/tips.shtml.

256. David Mikkelson, "Have Lightning Strikes Killed People Who Were Talking on the Phone?" *SNOPES*, July 5, 2010, http://www.snopes.com/horrors/techno/phone.asp.

257. Ker Than, "Cell Phones Increase Risk of Death By Lightning, Doctors Claim," *LiveScience,* June 22, 2006, http://www.livescience.com/843-cell-phones-increase-risk-death-lightning-doctors-claim.html.

258. Christopher Eild, "IARC Report to the Union for International Cancer Control (UICC) on the Interphone study," *International Agency for Research on Cancer, World Health Organization*, October 3, 2011, http://interphone.iarc.fr/UICC_Report_Final_03102011.pdf.

259. "Cell Phones and Cancer Risk," *National Cancer Institute*, https://www.cancer.gov/about-cancer/causes-prevention/risk/radiation/cell-phones-fact-sheet.

260. Mike M. Ahlers and Katia Hetter, "FCC votes to consider lifting in-flight cell phone ban," *CNN*, December 12, 2013, http://www.cnn.com/2013/12/12/travel/fcc-cell-phones-on-airplanes/; "FCC Allows Cell Phone Use on Flights," *ParkSleepFly,* October 10, 2014, http://www.parksleepfly.com/blog/cell-phones-on-planes/.

261. "Computer and Television Screens," *Epilepsy Action*, updated March 2015, https://www.epilepsy.org.uk/info/photosensitive-epilepsy/computer-television-screens.

262.   Howard J. Bennett, "Ever Wondered About the Lead in Pencils? Despite the name, They Have Never Been Made of Lead," *Washington Post*, November 30, 2014, https://www.washingtonpost.com/lifestyle/kidspost/ever-wondered-about-the-lead-in-pencils/2014/11/26/f8b5869c-548a-11e4-809b-8cc0a295c773_story.html?utm_term=.b33281ad0198.

263.   "Patients' Eyes Open Wide for Awake Brain Surgery," *Department of Anesthesiology, Ohio State University*, n.d., http://anesthesiology.osu.edu/article.cfm?ID=3259.

264.   "Injury Facts® 2016 Edition," *National Safety Council*, http://www.nsc.org/learn/safety-knowledge/Pages/injury-facts-chart.aspx.